WINNING CHESS
Piece by Piece

Ted Nottingham,
Bob Wade &
Al Lawrence

Sterling Publishing Co., Inc.
New York

Thanks go to:

CHARLES G. NURNBERG, a dynamic publisher, making available for the first time a series of books on the Lincolnshire Method.

CLAIRE BAZINET, an editor marvelously thorough and sensitive.

BOB WADE, O.B.E., whose international scholarship adds luster to this book.

AL LAWRENCE, who knows the American chess scene like no other.

FRANCIS BOWERS, for his help and terrific and conscientious proofreading.

MICHELLE BOWERS, for her typing of the original manuscript.

BARBARA BERKOWITZ, for her chess board photos.

Inspiration for "faction" stories and actual accounts in this book are appreciatively derived from many sources, including: the writings of Sir Martin Gilbert, Winston Churchill's official biographer; Werner Ring's *Life with the Enemy,* Doubleday, 1982 (Warsaw ghetto); *New York Times* music critic Harold C. Schonberg's *Grandmasters of Chess* (Philidor quotes about Bonnour), Jerzy Gizycki's *History of Chess* (Robespierre), and Daniel Fiske's classic book *Chess in Iceland.*

Library of Congress Cataloging-in-Publication Data

Nottingham, Ted.

    Winning chess piece by piece / Ted Nottingham, Bob Wade & Al Lawrence.

      p.   cm

    Includes index.

    Summary: Presents a series of chess puzzles organized around the pieces involved, covering knight, rook, bishop, and queen moves, forks, pins, and sacrifices, and surveying some of the game's grandmasters.

    ISBN 0-8069-9955-1

    1. Chess for children--juvenile literature. [1. Chess.] I. Wade, Robert Graham. II. Lawrence, Al. III. Title. IV. Title: Winning chess.

    GV1446.N69   1998

    794.1'2—dc21

                                 98-48171

                                   CIP

10 9 8 7 6 5 4 3 2   AC

First paperback edition published in 2000 by
Sterling Publishing Company, Inc.
387 Park Avenue South, New York, N.Y. 10016
© 1998 by Ted Nottingham, Bob Wade & Al Lawrence
Distributed in Canada by Sterling Publishing
c/o Canadian Manda Group, One Atlantic Avenue, Suite 105
Toronto, Ontario, Canada M6K 3E7
Distributed in Great Britain and Europe by Chris Lloyd
463 Ashley Road, Parkstone, Poole, Dorset, BH14 0AX, England
Distributed in Australia by Capricorn Link (Australia) Pty Ltd.
P.O. Box 6651, Baulkham Hills, Business Centre, NSW 2153, Australia
Manufactured in the United States of America

Sterling ISBN 0-8069-9955-1 Trade
                  0-8069-9970-5 Paper

CONTENTS

PART ONE

A GAME CALLED CHESS

The Chess-Playing Codebreakers

This England never did, nor never shall lie at the proud foot of a conqueror.

Shakespeare—*Richard II*

Every time you use a computer, remember the British chess-playing codebreakers who invented the world's first computers and who, by their skill and brilliance, broke Germany's wonder codes during World War II.

Headlines and radios screamed out the news. Just one salvo from the German battleship *Bismarck* had sunk Britain's pride, the *Hood*. If something wasn't done, the *Bismarck* would wander the vast Atlantic—able to hide like a needle in a haystack—and sink Allied ships!

Without delay, Winston Churchill, England's Prime Minister, phoned Bletchley Park, where Britain's chess players were working on coded messages sent out by Germany's marvelous "Enigma" machines. Churchill had called the chess players "my geese that laid the golden eggs" and he needed them now. He said, simply, "Decode any message about the *Bismarck*. There are twenty American convoys out there. The *Bismarck* will sink the lot."

Alan Turing and Hugh Alexander looked at one another. They had cracked the Enigma codes used by the German Air Force, but not those of its Navy. The rain and fog in the Atlantic meant that Allied ships could not even glimpse the *Bismarck*. And, no surprise, she was traveling under a cloak of radio silence.

Suddenly, the codebreakers had an amazing stroke of luck. A German Air Force Commander whose son was aboard the *Bismarck* used the Air Force code to ask where the ship was heading. Breathless, the codebreakers waited. The response came in the same "broken" code: "BREST." It was exactly what the codebreakers wanted to hear. They called Rapid Falls 4466, Churchill's phone number.

Some of the most marvelous inventions of the twentieth century resulted from the Second World War. The Germans gave the world rockets that took man to the moon, the Americans gave it nuclear power, but the young British chess players gave it perhaps the most important invention—the computers on which they deciphered Germany's codes.

P.S.: In *Independence Day*, an American film appropriately released on the 4th of July in 1966, a chess-playing codebreaker used a computer to defeat an alien invasion of Earth. A good film and great idea. But those British chess players are still considered the world's top codebreakers!

THE CODEBREAKERS

Hugh Alexander was captain of the British chess team at the 1939 Buenos Aires Olympiad. In l943, he and his friends Stuart Milner Barry and Harry Golombek helped crack the German Naval codes used in the Battle of the Atlantic. After the war, Alexander became head of Research and Development at Britain's Signals headquarters.

In the early 1950s, Alexander won a marathon 123-move game against the world's number 2-seeded David Bronstein. Of course, the game made headlines in Britain. One of Bronstein's positions was used in the James Bond film *From Russia with Love*.

Sir Stuart Milner Barry, who was also part of the Olympiad chess team, once went to see Churchill to explain the codebreakers' need for top priority. He didn't get in, but his message did. Churchill ordered, "See that they get all they want." From then on, Churchill saw and read Top Secret reports on the codebreakers' work every day.

Harry Golombek, also an Olympiad chess team member, later became chess correspondent of the London *Times*. In the late 1970s, he personally explained to the authors of this chess book the enormous help given by the codebreakers—help that enabled the Navy to locate and sink the *Bismarck*.

Alan Turing, the brilliant leader of the codebreakers, was not himself a top chess player. Tragically, he died a young man—at only 32 years of age. Still, he worked on one of the first computers ever designed to break codes, and after the war, devised an early chess computer program.

Gordon Welchman was the only top codebreaker who did not play chess.

Photo by Jim Woodward, Sebastian Studios, courtesy of the U.S. Chess Federation, New Windsor, NY 12553

An Historic Meeting

There is a tide in the affairs of men, which, taken at the flood, leads on to fortune.

Shakespeare—*Julius Caesar*

In August 1941, the U.S.S. *Augusta* lay in a bay just off the coast of Canada. On it, the American president, Franklin D. Roosevelt, was meeting Winston Churchill. The president wanted to learn more about the codebreakers and their wonderful computers. He and the British prime minister also wanted the world to know that Britain and America were friends and allies. There, on the deck of the *Augusta*, they signed the Atlantic Charter.

Two American destroyers escorted the ship Churchill was on as far as Iceland. The Arctic cold set him thinking. Churchill was delighted with the brilliant success of his codebreakers. He had read the Icelandic sagas and knew that chess came to Iceland about the year 1000. In London's British Museum he had seen the Lewis chess set. He recalled how, in 1831, the sea had suddenly uncovered these regal, mysterious pieces on the island of Lewis off the Scottish coast. Viking sailors had sailed the same route he had just taken and perhaps played chess in America a long time before Columbus came.

With the young men in London breaking Hitler's most secret codes, chess was a part of Churchill's life again. He mused how he had played as a young Army officer and how his own father, Lord Randolph, had founded the Oxford University Chess Club and played a good thirty-three-move game against Wilhelm Steinitz, the world champion.

Churchill was pleased with his meeting on board the *Augusta*. American experts were now with him to learn about the new British computers devised by his chess players. He prayed that Roosevelt would soon bring America to Britain's aid. A few weeks later, America entered the war firmly on Britain's side, and Churchill thanked God for this American president, the best friend Britain ever had.

Courtesy of U.S. Chess Federation, New Windsor, NY

Shown are faithful replicas of some of the famed Lewis set, with its wonderfully carved pieces: the king has his broadsword and the horses carrying the knights are ponylike. The "guard" on the right is the rook, or castle.

♖ ♖ **DID YOU KNOW?** ♖ ♖

Only recently, signs of a Viking fort, spectacular in size, were discovered on top of a remote promontory only a few yards from where the Lewis set was discovered in the island's dunes. A large Viking cemetery has since been discovered nearby.

Judith Polgar: Rose of Budapest

A very riband in the cap of youth.
                    Shakespeare—*Hamlet*

To nobody's surprise, when the World Chess Federation (FIDE) issued its 1996 ranking list, nineteen-year-old Judith Polgar was in the world's top ten. Since she became a grandmaster at fifteen—an even younger age than either Fischer or Kasparov achieved that lofty title—, Judith has steadily improved. Whether or not she ever plays Kasparov for the world title, she is a noted player and one of the most photographed young women in the world. Judith is the strongest female player since Vera Menchik, who was tragically killed when a Nazi V2 rocket landed on her home in London in 1944.

Judith achieved one of the most unusual victories of her career in the summer of 1995 in a tournament on the Isle of Lewis to commemorate the island's Viking past. Pieces were borrowed from museums in London and Edinburgh to display during the tournament. Judith finished first, ahead of British Grandmaster Nigel Short, who had played Kasparov for the world title at the Savoy, in London, in 1993.

In 1992, for $120,000, Judith played a match against the legendary former World Champion Boris Spassky, which she won convincingly. In 1998, she beat FIDE World Champion Anatoly Karpov in a rapid-play match. She also recently played and lost 2–1 to an IBM computer in a match of very quick games. But computers are very good at speed chess. Even Kasparov lost the first game of a 1996 match with "Deep Blue," the IBM computer, in Philadelphia, before winning three games to one. (Later, in 1997, he lost a match to the updated version of Deep Blue in New York City, 3½ to 2½, the first in which a reigning champion was defeated by a computer under tournament conditions.)

Susan Polgar

Judith Polgar's sisters are good players, too. Susan is the World Women's Chess Champion and Sophia, at fourteen, in 1989 played in Rome the best-ever tournament by a fourteen-year-old. The chess-playing Polgar family will do anything to help chess. In 1992, the sisters played for the United States Chess Federation at its U.S. CHESSathon in New York's Central Park to boost American interest in the game. Watch out for Judith and her sisters!

Photos by Jami L. Anson, courtesy of the U.S. Chess Federation

Judith Polgar

The First Grandmasters

Be great in act as you have been in thought.
Shakespeare—Richard II

Sailing for India in the year 1896, a 22-year-old Churchill wrote to his mother: "I have improved greatly since the voyage began, and I think I shall try to get really good at chess while I am in India." Like the young Churchill, every chess player wants to improve.

Who were the first grandmasters? In 1914 Nicholas II, last of the Romanovs and Czar of Russia, told the St. Petersburg Chess Club that he would personally give 1,000 rubles to the tournament's prize fund. Such a grand prize brought out the world's best players. Emanuel Lasker, the world champion, came to his first tournament in five years. The wonderful José Raúl Capablanca, who had learned to play at the age of four on his father's knee, came from Cuba. From Greenwich Village in New York City came Frank Marshall. Two years earlier, when Marshall made a brilliant twenty-third move in a game against Stepan Levitsky in Poland, spectators were said to have showered the board with gold pieces! Siegbert Tarrasch, a dogmatic German champion, came with devil-may-care Joseph Blackburne of England. There was also Akiba Rubinstein, who had just won five international tournaments in one year. From Russia came Ossip Bernstein and the young Alexander Alekhine, later to be world champion.

It was a triumph for the world champions. Lasker won by half a point over Capablanca, who became, after the First World War, the next champion. Alexander Alekhine, who dethroned Capablanca in 1927, came in third. Then came Tarrasch and Marshall. It was at the banquet after the match that the Czar, speaking in French, named those five players *grandmaîtres*, or "grandmasters," and the term came into general use. But earlier great players, like the American champion Paul Morphy, are considered grandmasters too, even if they played before the time of Czar Nicholas II.

Today, chess players have to score well in three very strong tournaments before they are entitled to the title of grandmaster—which is officially given now by the World Chess Federation. Maybe someday you will follow in the footsteps of the first grandmasters.

Emanuel Lasker   **José Raúl Capablanca**

Courtesy of the U.S.C.F., New Windsor, NY

Ron Atkinson drawing, courtesy of the U.S.C.F.

♛♛DID YOU KNOW? ♛♛

In 1890, the New York City police arrested World Champion Wilhelm Steinitz! Steinitz was playing a chess match by telegram with Russian master Mikhail Tchigorin, who was in Havana, Cuba. The officers thought the written chess moves were a secret code!

The Battleground

Chess is fought on an 8-by-8-square board. The earliest board games, such as Sennet, which was found in the tombs of the Egyptian pharaoh Tutankhamen, were played on a smaller board. Much more recently, but still some time ago, in the 1930s World Champion Capablanca proposed a 10-by-10-square board with new pieces, one an "Ambassador," which would be allowed to move like both a queen *and* a knight. His ideas, however, were not taken up, so the 8-by-8-square chess board survives...and provides plenty of pleasure still.

THE CHESS BOARD

Each square of the board can be named. We use the simplest system—called algebraic. It is based on the first eight letters of the alphabet —**a**, **b**, **c**, **d**, **e**, **f**, **g**, **h**—and the numbers **1** through **8**.

The right-hand-corner square nearest the player with the white pieces is **h1**—the junction of the **h** column (or "file") and row **1** (or "rank"). Nearest to black's right hand is **a8**. Try naming some squares. For example, **d4** is where the **d** file and rank **4** meet.

By custom, the white chessmen are always set up along ranks **1** and **2** and the black along **7** and **8**.

BLACK PLAYER

WHITE PLAYER

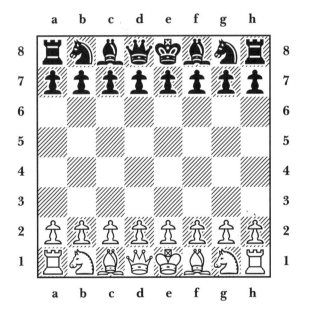

Always set up the board with a white square on the right-hand corner. Remember, "White on right."

Doing the Piece Mazes

The ancient Greeks created myths we remember to this day. One famous story tells of King Minos of Crete, whose son was born half bull and half man. Minos turned to the extraordinary skill of the Greek Daedalus to build a maze to hide his hideous son. Daedalus had a reputation for invention—having built wings for himself and his son to fly.

Real-life ancient Greek writers like Plato describe a board game based purely on skill as being widely played. The first great players of chess were the Arabs, but perhaps the Greeks really did invent a forerunner of chess as well as construct their magnificent buildings and statues—and of course Daedalus' maze!

In honor of Greek invention and British codebreaking genius, we include here a series of tests based on Daedalus' maze. Your challenge is to find your way through each maze, using chess codebreaker skill. You are given different tasks with each piece, based on how the pieces move. Once you have worked out and passed the tests, fill in the certificate provided, which has been signed by all of us (chess teacher Ted Nottingham; Al Lawrence, former Executive Director of the U.S. Chess Federation; and Bob Wade, O.B.E., England's Chief Trainer). You've earned it!

Later in this book, too, we show you how to rate your chess play and that of your friends. We have also provided you with a special age/grade progress chart so that you can compare yourself with the world's best—only in fun, perhaps, but we hope you enjoy it!

Chess Notation

Chess moves are written in notation, a way of writing out the moves that can look very much like some strange code. This code, however, is easy to break and is not a secret. Chess players around the world know and use some variety of notation. Once you know the board and follow the games in this book, you will be able to read notation, too. It will allow you to be able to replay your own games (if you write your moves down as you make your moves) or to play against opponents by mail, no matter where they are.

The basics of chess notation are the coordinates of the board (the file letters and rank numbers, such as **d2** and **h7**) and the use of one or more of the following symbols:

Notation	Meaning
–	moves to
×	takes
+	check
++	double check
#	checkmate
!	a good move
?	a bad move
0–0	short castle
0–0–0	long castle

Notation may be written in different ways. Sometimes the name of the piece is not given; sometimes the piece name is written but only the landing square and not the take-off square is given. And, oh yes, the letter **N** stands for Knight. Why? Because **K** is used for King!

Piece Values

In the piece mazes in this book, you'll be asked to tour the board to capture your opponent's pieces. Nevertheless, we want to remind you here that knowing when to capture, or "take," in chess—and when *not* to—is one of the most important decisions you need to make, and get right, in playing chess. Quite often, your decision as to whether or not to take a piece will be determined by the swap, or trade, value.

TRADE VALUE OF THE PIECES

PAWN (P) ♟ = ♟ (1)

KNIGHT (N) ♞ = ♟ ♟ ♟ (3)

BISHOP (B) ♝ = ♟ ♟ ♟ (3)

ROOK (R) ♜ = ♟ ♟ ♟ ♟ ♟ (5)

QUEEN (Q) ♛ = ♟ ♟ ♟ ♟ ♟ ♟ ♟ ♟ (9)

Of course, the KING (K) ♚ is PRICELESS!

♞♞ DID YOU KNOW? ♞♞

The 1972 Spassky (St. Petersburg, U.S.S.R.) and Fischer (New York, U.S.A) world championship match in Iceland was the world's most publicized chess match. Played at the height of the Russian–American cold war, the match was covered by nearly every major newspaper in the world.

Based on the piece values here, in the game below would you take the black rook with the white queen? Is it a good idea?

The answer is no! Why? Let's see.

Qc2 × Rc6 (remember, × means takes)

Look here. If you take the rook with your queen, then your opponent can take your queen with the pawn! A rook is worth five points; a queen, nine. So you win five, but lose nine: a bad bargain!

..... b7 × c6 (..... means Black's move)

A bad bargain for White!

PART TWO

THE ROOK

The Rook's Maze

American football has "running backs" and soccer has "flying wingers." The rook is the running back or flying winger of the chess board!

The rook moves in straight lines as many squares as he likes, but he cannot jump! To capture, he simply lands on an enemy piece and "takes" it.

ROOK TAKES FOURTEEN

Set up your board as shown. The black pieces are fixed; they do not move. You are allowed fourteen moves with the white rook. Can you take everything on the board?

Before you start, just look over the pieces in their maze positions. It's a good idea not to touch pieces until you have *seen your way* through the maze—the whole way around.

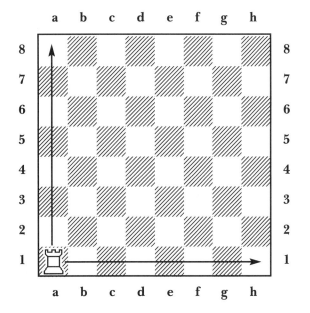

Remember, you must capture *on every move*! The white rook in the maze must take all fourteen black pieces on the board, one right after another, in just fourteen moves. In these learning mazes, you do not take turns—first White and then Black. It is your turn all the time.

So, let's start. We'll give you the first moves, and when you finish, look at the solution given upside down below.

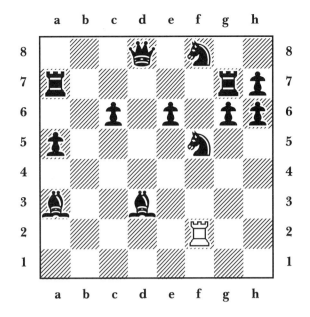

The first plays are:

Rh2 × f2

and

Rf2 × f5

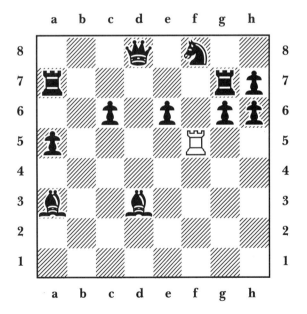

Solution (simple notation): R × f2, × f5, × f8, × d8, × d3, × a3, × a5, × a7, × g7, × h7, × h6, × g6, × e6, × c6

AHOY, MATE-Y!

On July 1, 1996, the U.S. Navy aircraft carrier *Intrepid*, retired and moored in New York harbor, first played host to the annual United States Chess Federation CHESSathon. For several hundred young chess enthusiasts playing beneath the ship's impressive battlements and the wings of aircraft, it was indeed a day to remember.

All photos by Tom LaBarbara and Jami L. Anson, courtesy of the U.S. Chess Federation, New Windsor, NY 12553

Mating Race

If it were done when 'tis done, then 'twere well it were done quickly.

Shakespeare—*Macbeth*

Apopular game is the mating race. Can you get a checkmate more quickly than your friend? It goes this way. Both of you are given the same pieces, the same position. First one of you tries to give checkmate, then the other.

The winner is the player who completes the checkmate in the least number of moves.

First, we show you how two rooks build up a checkmating net.

TWO ROOKS VS. KING

Here is part of a race to checkmate. As you do it, you'll see how little snags crop up. Nevertheless, the pattern of the rooks taking turns advancing on each side is what you want.

This is the starting position for the race. After you go through the moves here, see if you can do it more quickly on your own.

1 Ra1 – a4

This cuts the black king off from ranks 1 through 4.

1 ..... Kd5 – e5

The black king stays as long as it can on the fifth rank.

2   Rh1 – h5+ (check)

The two rooks work together. Now the black king is being forced back to **d6**.

2 ..... Ke5 – d6

Can you see what's happening? Now the "a" rook will come to the attack.

3   Ra4 – a6+

Now ranks 1 to 6 are cut off to the black king.

3   .....   Kd6 – d7

The pattern is now clear. It will be the turn of the "h" rook.

4   Rh5 – h7+

Now the black king's field is roped off. He has only rank 8 left.

4 ..... Kd7 – d8

5 Ra6 – a8 checkmate

There is nowhere left to go. It's checkmate!

Now, it's your turn. Think you can do it? In fewer moves? Look back to page 15 and set up the same starting position again, then try it on your own.

TEST YOUR PROGRESS

Here is another starting position. Can you get this checkmate?

Solution: 1. Kf3 Kd3 2. Rd1+ Kc3 3. Ke3 Kc4 4. Rc2+ Kb3 5. Kd3 Kb4 6. Rb1+ Ka3 7. Kc2 Ka4 8. Ra2++

The Rook That Grinds
Like a Mill

A foregone conclusion.

Shakespeare—*Othello*

Just watch the rook on **g7** at right take everything on the seventh rank, and then even the rook on **a8**!

1 Rg7 × e7+

This kind of check is called "discovered check." The rook has moved and we then discover that the king is in check from the bishop on **b2**. Discovered check is one of the most explosive weapons in chess, because the "uncovering" piece can do anything it wants without being taken!

1 ..... Kh8 – g8

This is the king's only move, and on this discovered check you will see the whole pattern of the "rook that grinds like a mill."

2 Re7 – g7+

The rook checks again, forcing the king into the corner, where he will be ready for another discovered check from the bishop on **b2**!

2 ..... Kg8 – h8

The king is now resting on the diagonal of the bishop at **b2**. The rook now has a free, dangerous move that will leave this bishop checking the king.

3 Rg7 × c7+

The free move! Of course the king is in check from that bishop.

3 ..... Kh8 – g8

Forced—it's the only move!

4 Rc7 – g7+

The rook returns to check. The king will have to step onto that diagonal again. The bishop checks. The rook grinds like a mill.

4 ..... Kg8 – h8

Now for that free move. Which one would you make?

5 Rg7 × b7+

The rook takes another piece, and the king is again in check from the bishop on **b2**. Are you seeing the pattern?

5 ..... Kh8 – g8

The king has to do this—it's forced!

6 Rb7 – g7+

The check comes; the king has to go to **h8**.

6 ..... Kg8 – h8

Look high or low, the rook has only the pawn on **a7** to take.

7 Rg7 × a7+

The black king is forced again move out of check.

Now the way is clear for White to take Black's rook on **a8**.

After taking the rook, White has a position with king, rook, bishop, and pawns against Black's king, knight, and pawn—a very big, winning advantage.

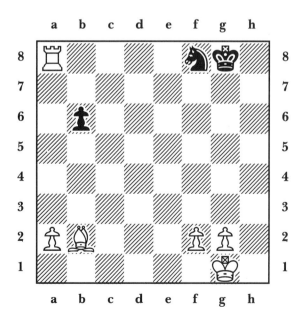

Can You Grind Like a Mill?

Can you get your rook on **g7** to the enemy's rook on **a8**, taking the queen on **e7**, the pawn on **c7**, the knight on **b7,** and the pawn on **a7** on the way?

Solution: 1. R × e7+ Kg8 2. Rg7+ Kh8 3. R × c7+ Kg8 4. Rg7+ Kh8 5. R × b7+ Kg8 6. Rg7+ Kh8 7. R × a7+ Kg8 8. R × a8

QUICK QUIZ

Look carefully here. Should the white pawn at **c4** take the black pawn?

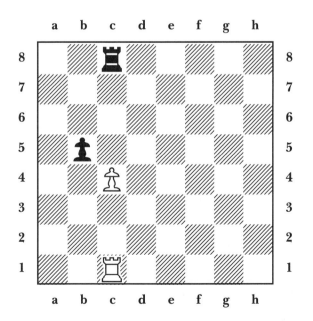

Solution: Beware! The answer is "No!" because the white pawn is *pinned*. If it takes the black pawn, look: ..... Rc8 × Rc1.

PART THREE

KNIGHT Vs. BISHOP

He doth nothing but talk of his horse.
                    Shakespeare—*The Merchant of Venice*

The Knight's Maze

In the knight's advanced driving test below, the white knight has to take the sixteen black and white pawns set up on both sides of the board. How many moves do you think it will take to do that? Hint: It takes 18 moves to take one set of eight pawns.

This is the way that we have found to do the knight's advanced driving test. The first move is:

1 Ng1 – f3

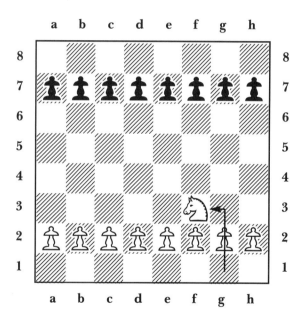

Remember, in this practice driving test, you move only the knight and you can capture pawns of either color.

2 Nf3 – g5

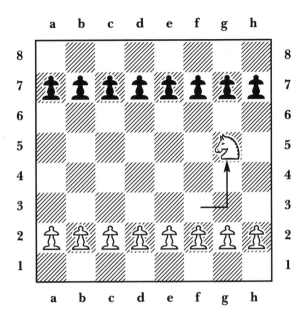

3 Ng5 × h7

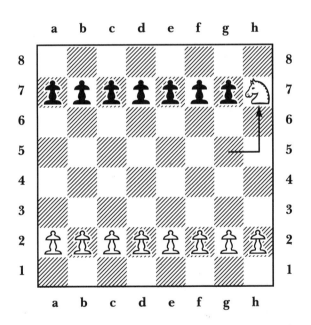

4 Nh7 – g5

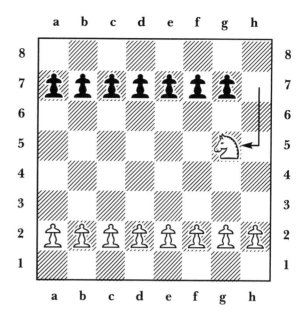

5 Ng5 × f7

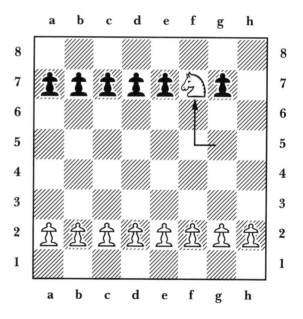

6 Nf7 – e5

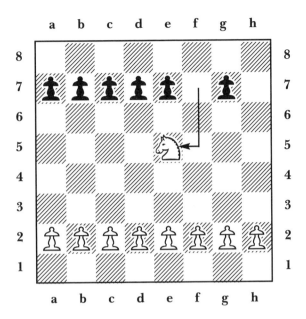

7 Ne5 × d7

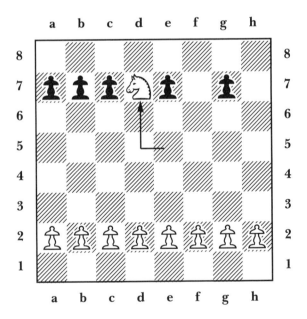

8 Nd7 – c5

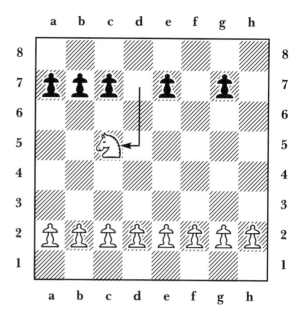

9 Nc5 × b7

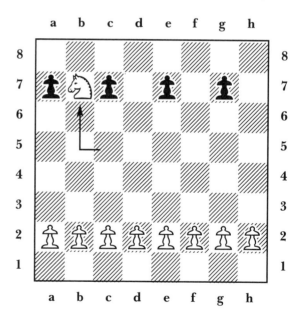

Now, to get the black pawn on **a7**, the knight has to make a three-point turn. This is how it's done.

10 Nb7 – a5

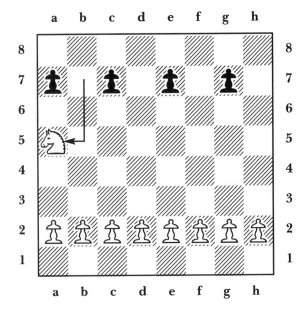

11 Na5 – c6

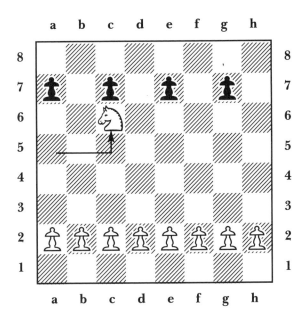

12 Nc6 × a7

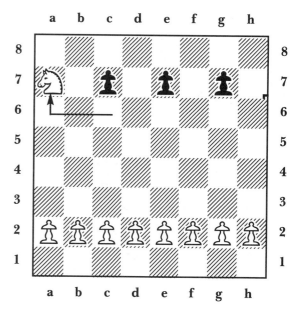

So the three-point turn looks like this.

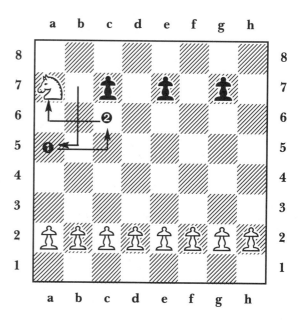

Then, from **a7**, the knight moves to **b5**, **c7**, **d5**, **e7** and **f5**, and we pick it up again with the white knight taking the last black pawn

18 Nf5 × g7

Total so far: 18 moves. But we still have to go back across the board and take the eight white pawns.

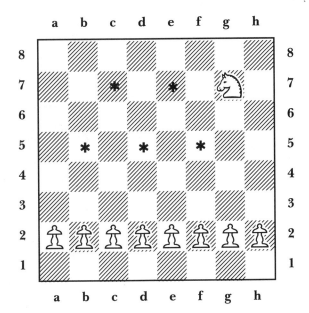

19 Ng7 – h5

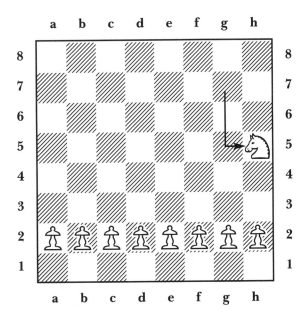

20 Nh5 – f4

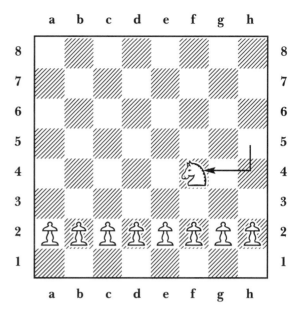

21 Nf4 × g2

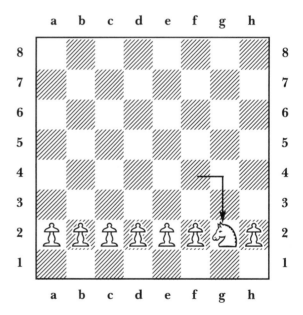

From **g2**, the knight moves to **f4**, **e2**, **d4**, **c2**, to **b4**, taking two more of the white pawns.

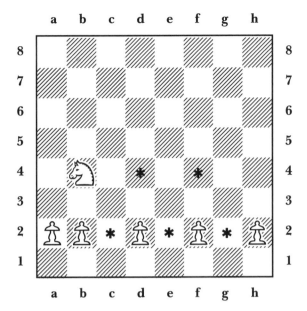

27 Nb4 × a2

Now, here we need to make another three-point turn, to get that pawn on **b2**.

Before we go on, look at the board and see if you can find three moves that will allow you to take the pawn on **b2** on the third move.

By the way, can you possibly take that pawn on the *second* move?

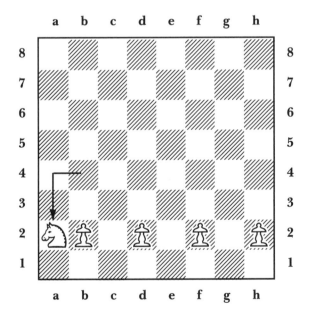

No, you need three moves to make the turn and get the **b4** pawn. Two moves won't do!

So, here we give you:

28 Na2 – b4

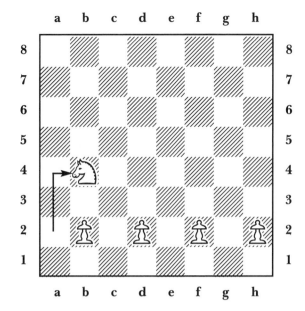

29 Nb4 – d3

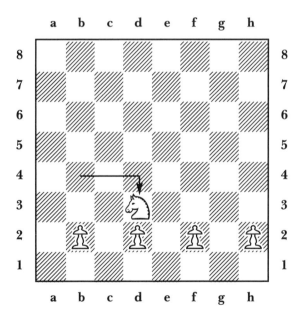

30 Nd3 × b2

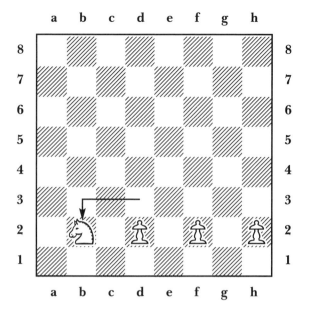

That's one three-point turn. Did you see a different one, when you looked at the board with the knight on **a2** (page 34)? Maybe this one?

Or this one?

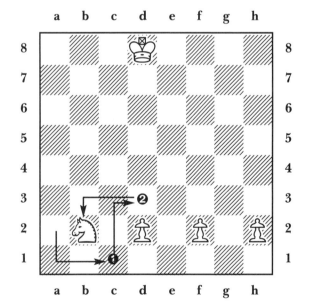

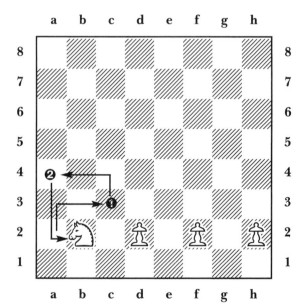

Now, let's mop up the rest of the pawns.

31 Nb2 – c4

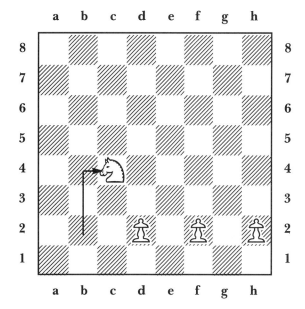

Then, **d2**, **e4**, and **f2**.

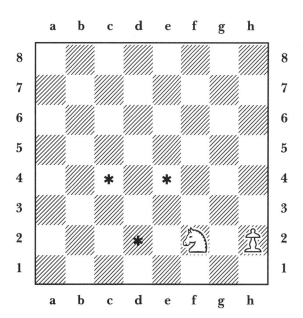

That last pawn is easy.

35 Nf2 – g4

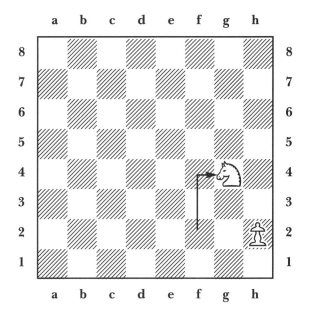

36 Ng4 × h2

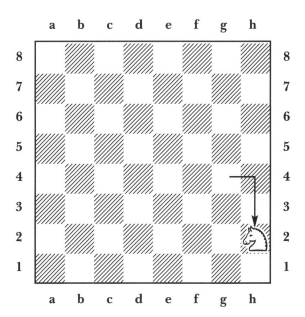

Now, can you set up a chess board and take all the pawns with the white knight? If you can, you have conquered the advanced driving test, the Knight's Maze!

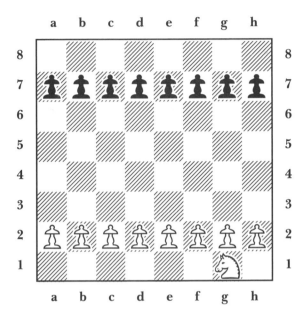

Our solution is provided at right. Are there other ways to do the knight's advanced driving test maze? Can you do it in fewer moves? Is it possible?

KNIGHT'S MAZE MOVES

1	Ng2 – f3
2	Nf3 – g5
3	Ng5 × h7
4	Nh7 – g5
5	Ng5 × f7
6	Nf7 – e5
7	Ne5 × d7
8	Nd7 – c5
9	Nc5 × b7
10	Nb7 – a5
11	Na5 – c6
12	Nc6 × a7
13	Na7 – b5
14	Nb5 × c7
15	Nc7 – d5
16	Nd5 × e7
17	Ne7 – f5
18	Nf5 × g7
19	Ng7 – h5
20	Nh5 – f4
21	Nf4 × g2
22	Ng2 – f4
23	Nf4 × e2
24	Ne2 – d4
25	Nd4 × c2
26	Nc2 – b4
27	Nb4 × a2
28	Na2 – b4
29	Nb4 – d3
30	Nd3 × b2
31	Nb2 – c4
32	Nc4 × d2
33	Nd2 – e4
34	Ne4 × f2
35	Nf2 – g4
36	Ng4 × h2

The Bishop's Maze

Make assurance double sure.

Shakespeare—*Macbeth*

On the board below are fourteen pieces for you to take with the white bishop—waiting for you on **g2**. Remember, work all the moves out in your mind's eye before you begin. Later on, try setting up such mazes—all sorts of numbers of pieces—for your bishop to take. These types of exercise are good practice for thinking moves out ahead in a real game.

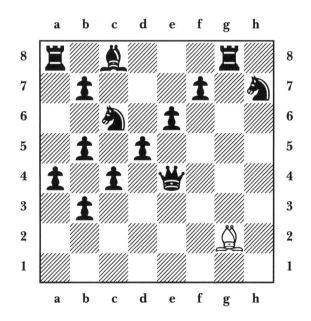

Let's do a few moves together to start, then you can go on on your own.

1 B × e4

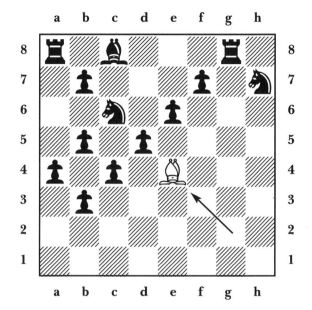

2 B × h7

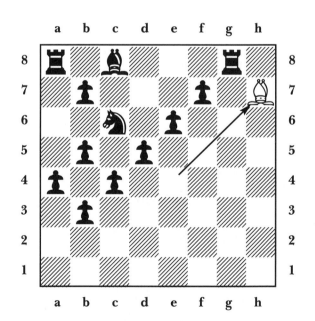

3 B × g8

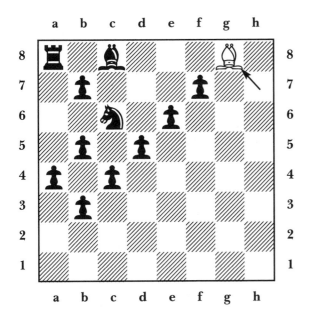

Now, finish up this bishop's advanced driving test. When you're done, check the solution below.

Solution: 1. B × e4 2. B × h7 3. B × g8 4. B × f7 5. B × e6 6. B × c8 7. B × b7 8. B × a8 9. B × c6 10. B × d5 11. B × c4 12. B × b5 13. B × a4 14. B × b3

Test Your Progress 1

On this maze are fifteen black pieces for the bishop to take. Can you work your way around the board in your mind's eye before you begin? It's good to be able to "read" the entire board when you play. See the solution below.

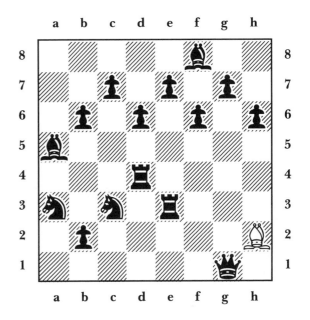

Solution: 1. B × g1 2. B × e3 3. B × h6 4. B × g7 5. B × f8 6. B × e7 7. B × f6 8. B × d4 9. B × c3 10. B × b2 11. B × a3 12. B × d6 13. B × c7 14. B × b6 15. B × a5

TEST YOUR PROGRESS 2

Here is another, similar, maze of fifteen pieces, this time for the black bishop to take. As you did before, plan out each move around the board in your mind before you start out. Compare your solution with the one given below.

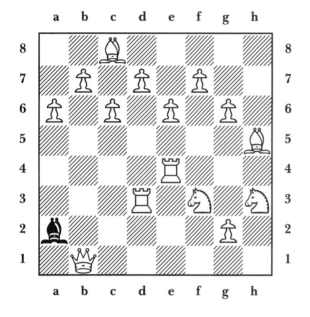

Solution: 1. B × b1 2. B × d3 3. B × a6 4. B × b7 5. B × c8 6. B × d7 7. B × c6 8. B × e4 9. B × f3 10. B × g2 11. B × h3 12. B × e6 13. B × f7 14. B × g6 15. B × h5

All four photos by Jim Woodward, Sebastian Studios, courtesy of the U.S. Chess Federation, New Windsor, NY 12553

Bishop or Knight?

Which is better: the bishop or the knight? This question spells out one of the great arguments of chess. Everyone knows the queen is the strongest, and after her the rook. But people disagree when it comes to the bishop and the knight. With the diagonals clear, the bishop is strong. However, the knight's ability to jump is valuable when everything else is blocked.

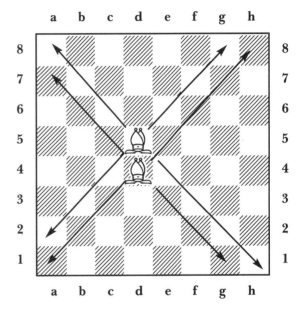

Experienced players often prefer the bishop pair. As the game goes on, the board clears and they become stronger and stronger. To help you make up your own mind about the question, on the next few pages let us compare the moves of the two pieces in different board positions.

Example 1

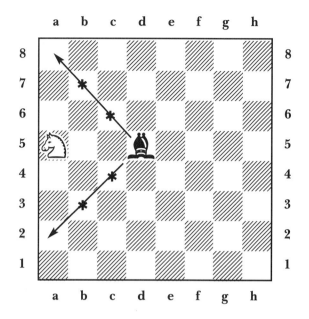

Example 2

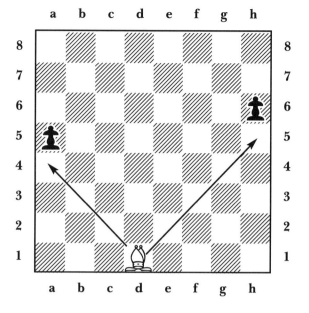

The bishop has trapped the knight at the side of the board. All its escape squares are covered by the bishop. While the bishop can do this, there is nothing similar for the knight.

These two black pawns are ready to advance. They are on opposite sides of the board, yet they still cannot get past the bishop, whose power along the diagonals stops both of them. The knight, with his shorter move, could not possibly do this.

Example 3

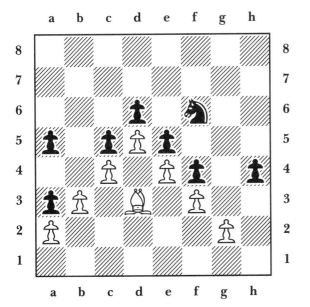

Example 4

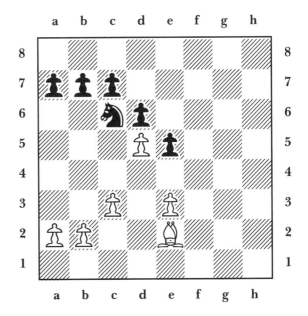

This is when the bishop is weak. The bishop stands on a white diagonal but is blocked by his own pawns. He can't take his own pieces. And the bishop can't jump over pieces. So he's in a prison made by his own army! With the pawns blocking the white squares, the knight is much more dangerous.

Be careful of this! Here, the bishop isn't blocked by his pawns, so he's dangerous! The white pawn has just moved to **d5**. Attacked by it, the knight has to move.

Example 5

Example 6

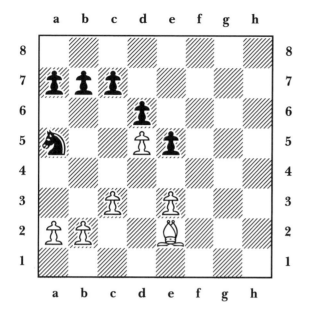

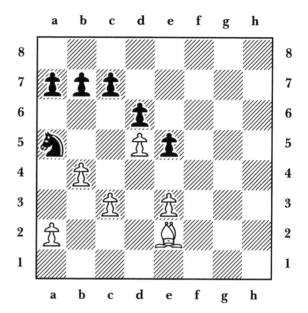

A knight's move to the side of the board is generally not as good as one to the center. Why? Because on the side of the board, the knight can only go in one direction. After all, he cannot jump off the board!

Here, the further squares are all guarded by either the white "a" pawn or the bishop.

The pawn on **b2** goes to **b4** and the knight is trapped against the edge of the board.

Have another look at the previous diagram, at left, and suggest another move. How about, maybe, Black moving **..... Nc6 – e7**? With that move, the knight cannot be trapped. Right?

Place the Knight Well

Let us see where the knight is best placed.

In the corner of the chess board, the knight covers only two squares.

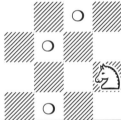

One square from the corner, the knight still covers only three squares.

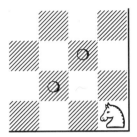

Two squares along from the corner, and the knight covers four squares.

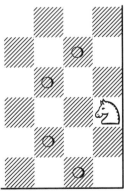

One *file* in from the side of the board and now well away from the corner, the knight covers six squares.

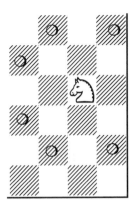

In the center of the board the knight covers eight squares. When you are playing chess, always ask yourself, "Where is the best place for my knight?" However, the right answer can depend on other pieces.

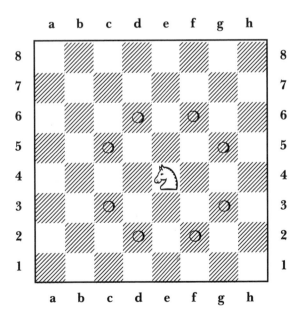

Chess Forks

A "fork in the road" means that the road splits, becoming two roads. In chess, a "fork" means *two* pieces are attacked by *one*. The trick is the placement of the attacking piece.

Look at the positions of the pieces below. This is a "family" knight fork. The black knight forks not only the king and queen, but the rook as well!

Here, the knight attacks both the king and the queen. Can you see the fork?

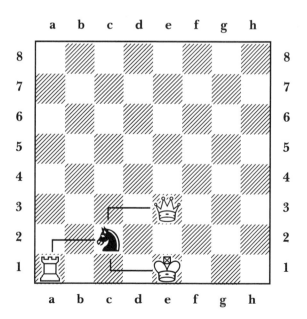

Bishop Fork...and Other Good Things

Bishops, which move diagonally on straight paths, can also attack effectively with forks.

Here, the black bishop "forks" the king and the rook. Since White *must* move the king out of check, the bishop will take the rook.

With an X-ray attack, also called a *skewer*, a piece "sees through" a piece to get one behind it. Here, the white bishop on **b2** checks the king.

After the king is moved—which it *has* to be —the bishop will take the queen.

The black bishop attacks the knight on **d5**, which cannot move, as that would leave the king in check. The knight is *pinned* in place.

In the next move, the bishop will take the knight. The white king is too far away to help.

Bishop Vs. Knight Game

Set up the pawns on the board, with a white bishop placed at **c1** and a black knight at **b8**.

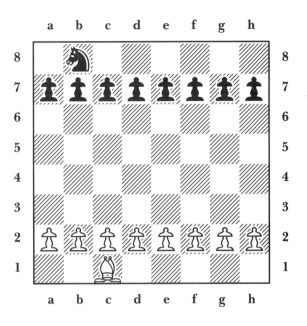

The rule of the game is simple: The first to get a pawn through to the far side wins. *However*, the pawn must *not* be captured immediately following its arrival on the far side.

We'll let you complete this game on your own, but here is the first move to start you off right…

1 d2 – d3

…and a hint. Place the white pawns on squares of opposite color to the bishop. If you block your own bishop with pawns, the game will soon be lost.

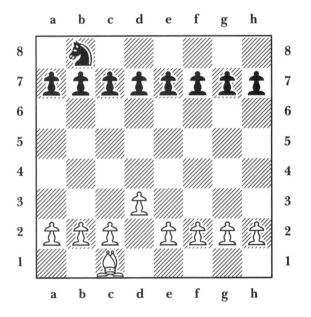

As you play, look for moves that cut down the knight's freedom to move. The knight in the position shown here would be taken by a pawn if it moved forward to any square. So move the bishop—and block the knight.

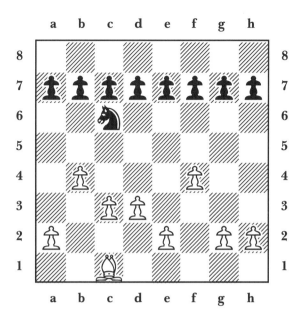

Here's another game to play:

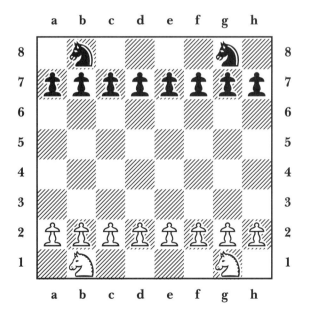

And another:

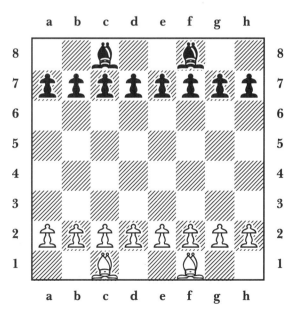

Noah's Ark Trap

We have seen the knight trapped at the far side of the board, so it is only fair to show a bishop hemmed in and trapped. So many people for so long have been caught by this trick that it is known as the "Noah's Ark Trap."

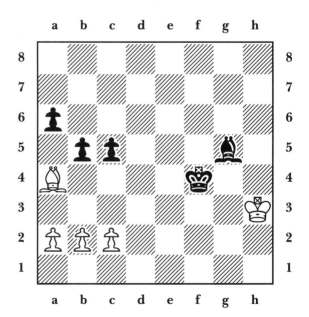

Here, the white bishop is stuck against the side of the board, where it has few moves, and it's Black's turn.

The black pawn moves to **b5**.

The bishop moves back to **b3**. Can you see how the bishop is going to be trapped?

The black "c" pawn has moved to **c4**. The white bishop is now trapped. At the side of the board, it is very easy to get your pieces trapped!

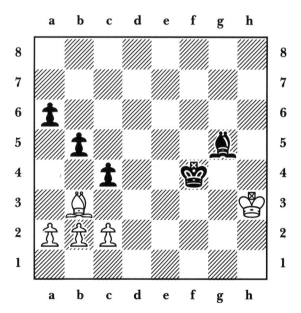

Jonathan Penrose: King of Knights

Give him all kindness: I had rather have such men my friends, than enemies.

Shakespeare—*Julius Caesar*

Britain's Nigel Short challenged Garry Kasparov for the world championship at the Savoy Theatre in London in 1993, and in 1996 was in the top 10 ranking list of the world—but some judges would give the honor of Britain's top player *ever* to Jonathan Penrose.

In 1960, at age twenty-seven, Penrose beat the then-world champion Mikhail Tal in a brilliant game. Since Tal is one of the best-ever world champions, this was an outstanding performance. Unfortunately, Penrose did not concentrate on a chess career, so is one of the might-have-beens of chess. He was, however, British champion ten times during the twelve-year period from 1958 to 1969.

To illustrate for you the wonderful talent of Jonathan Penrose, we present to you, on the following pages, a game played by seventeen-year-old Penrose against Walter Veitch in the 1950 British championship. It is a such a beautiful game—full of knight forks! You would do well to memorize it.

A Penrose Knight-Fork Game

	WHITE	BLACK
	Veitch	Penrose
1	d2 – d4	Ng8 – f6
2	c2 – c4	e7 – e6
3	Ng1 – f3	d7 – d5
4	g2 – g3	d5 × c4
5	Nb1 – d2	c7 – c5
6	d4 × c5	Bf8 × c5

7 Bf1 – g2

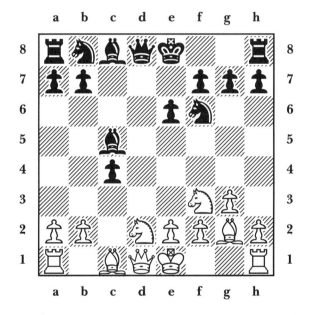

White is playing too passively.

Penrose is black and it is his move. He now begins a decisive attack based on knight forks. Just watch the damage done by his knight, now on **f6**.

7 ..... Bc5 × f2+

Penrose's bishop darts in to take a pawn and also gives check to the white king.

8 Ke1 × f2

Walter Veitch, an experienced player, must have wondered at the young Penrose's move. He takes the bishop.

8 ..... Nf6 – g4+

The black knight comes in to do its damage.

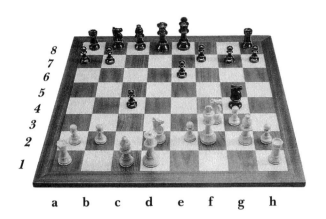

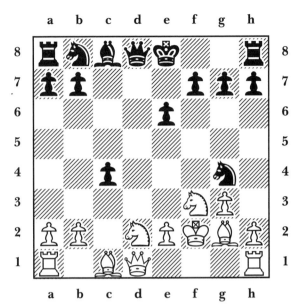

Now let us look at a few *possible* moves before we look at the move Veitch actually played.

9 Kf2 – f1

If Veitch had played this, then he would have been in for a nasty shock.

9 ..... Ng4 – e3+

The black knight forks the king, queen, and bishop—a kind of "family fork." This is why Veitch did *not* play **kf2 – f1**.

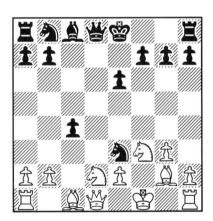

9 Kf2 – g1

If Veitch had played this…

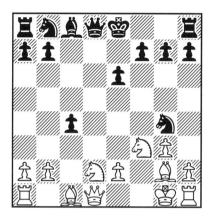

9 ..... Qd8 – b6+

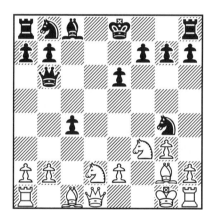

If the pawn blocks the check by going to **e3**, the queen just takes it and White has the same problem. Then…

10 Kg1 – f1 Qb6 – f2 checkmate

The king cannot get to **g1** or **e1** because of the black queen. The king cannot take the queen, because it is protected by that knight.

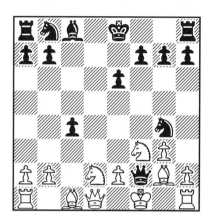

Back to the game: So Veitch's *actual* play was to move his king back to **e1**.

9 Kf2 – e1

9 ..... Ng4 – e3

The knight forks the queen and the bishop. But the knight is only after the big fish...the queen.

10 Qd1 – a4+

Amazingly, this check was the only safe move Veitch's queen could give. But it is not safe for long!

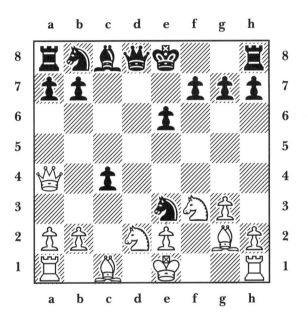

10 ..... Bc8 – d7

The bishop blocks the check and attacks the queen. What now for the queen?

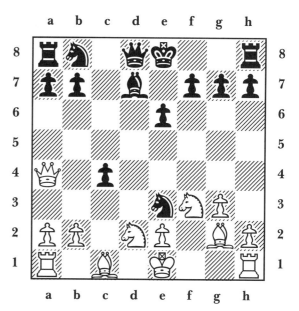

Say, this is played:

11 Qa4 – b4

The queen moves onto one of only two squares where she is not attacked (b4 or a3). But either square she chooses would have the same result.

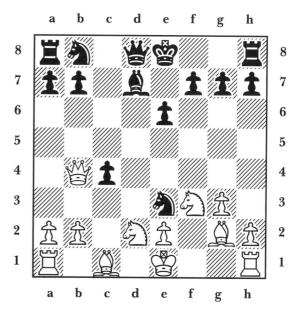

Now! The knight...

11 ..... Ne3 – c2+

The knight makes a family fork. King, rook, and queen are all included. After the king moves, Jonathan Penrose would obviously take the queen. Walter Veitch quickly saw, in the game, the damage that would be done after he had played his king back to **e1,** and so he resigned. A beautiful game!

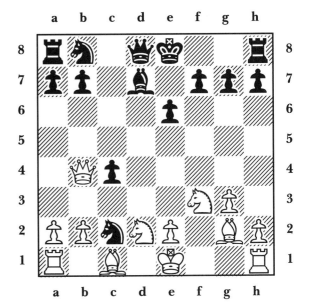

This is the journey of Penrose's knight. Some knight! Some journey!

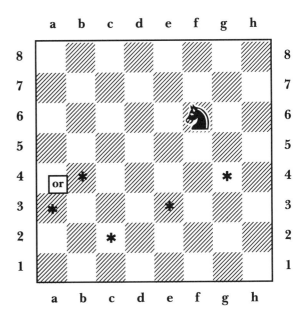

TEST YOUR PROGRESS

Can you see how to move the knight here, so that it will fork?

And also, here? See solutions below.

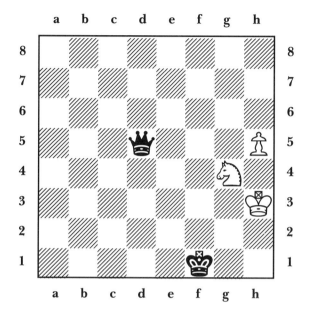

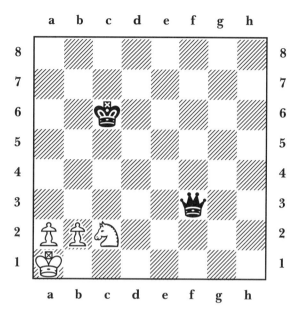

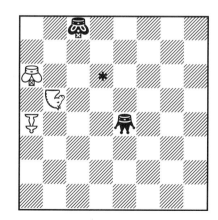

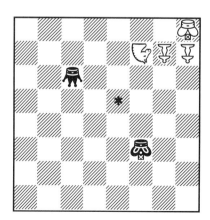

The Blindfold King: Philidor

The weakest go to the wall.

Shakespeare—*Romeo and Juliet*

Today Garry Kasparov plays world championship chess in really glitzy places like the Savoy Theatre in London or the top floor of New York's World Trade Center. But from 1750 to 1830, the Café de la Régence in Paris was the place to be for chess players. Through clouds of drifting smoke, you might see the great Napoleon, or Benjamin Franklin, one of the signers of the American Declaration of Independence, playing chess.

One charmingly unusual man was a Monsieur Bonnour, who always came with his little dog which, when his master was playing, "put his forepaws on the edge of the table, looking fiercely at each move of the opponent, showing its teeth and barking furiously if his master's opponent should win."

One of the most famous chess players of the time was the café's resident professional, Daniel Harrwitz, but he is not to be copied. He paid people to blow smoke into your face if you were playing him, and when the American Paul Morphy complained once of losing a move, Harrwitz rang the waiter's bell and ordered the man to look for a move as Mr. Morphy had just lost one.

It was into this café that chess's first great genius, André Philidor, came in the 1750s. He was born into a family of musicians; many of his relatives are listed in music encyclopedias. His music was lively and bright. Into his opera *Tom Jones*—the New York music critic Harold C. Schonberg notes in his book *Grandmasters of Chess*—Philidor introduced such sounds as the hunting horn, horses's hooves, and the crack of whips.

But though Philidor was an accomplished musician, he was also a chess player who could not only beat the world's best but play three games at once—blindfolded! Londoners marveled, seeing the trick as one of the greatest feats the human mind could accomplish.

In memory of this great Frenchman, who taught us that "pawns are the soul of chess," in this chapter we show you how to win when you have only a king and pawn left against your opponent's king. Remember that the pawn can become a queen if it reaches the other side of the board, so it is very important to know how to shepherd your pawn through.

The King's Royal Duel

First, for the duel, let's set up the two kings at opposite ends of the "e" line: the white king at **e1** and the black king **e8**.

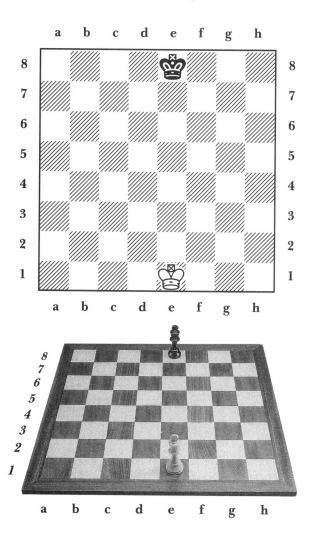

In this duel between the two kings, the first through to the other side of the board wins. Remember, the king moves only one square at a time, but can move in any direction. White always starts first.

1   Ke1 – e2

White, starting first, should get to the other end first. The skill for the black player will be to block it. You take up the challenge and take the black side.

White is now only six squares away from winning. You are seven. If you are going to have any hope with the black king, you must block the white one.

1 ..... Ke8 – e7

Six each now. But Black would be foolish to try to outrun the white king.

2 Ke2 – e3

Five to go now!

2 ..... Ke7 – d7

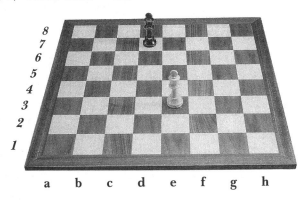

Black gives up trying to win the race across the board and plans to block the white king.

3 Ke3 – e4

The white king continues his march. Only four moves to the other side.

3 ..... Kd7 – e6

A very good move. Remember the king is so important that it is not allowed to be put where it can be taken. The white king is not permitted to go next to the black one. So the way forward is blocked. The white king cannot advance.

4 Ke4 – f4

Still four squares away. But your black king is five squares away and there is no point in trying to race.

4 ….. Ke6 – f6

Again your king blocks the way.

5 Kf4 – e4

Because the way forward is blocked, the white king is forced sideways. What will you do as Black, now?

5 ….. Kf6 – e6

Rightly, Black continues to block. Maybe White will retreat.

Now go back to after Black's second move (**1. Ke1 – e2 Ke8 – e7 2. Ke2 – e3 Ke7 – d7**), shown above, and take the White side. See if you can win by *using the move* **3 Ke3 – f4** *here*. You should.

Put the kings, again, at **e1** and **e8**. After some practicing, you should realize that, when White starts, White *always wins*. It's not a fair duel!

1.	e1	e2	e4	e5
2.	e1	e2	f4	e5
3.	e1	e2	d4	e5
4.	e1	e2	f3	e4	e5
5.	e1	e2	f3	f4	e5
6.	e1	e2	d3	d4	e5
7.	e1	e2	d3	e4	e5
8.	e1	f2	g3	f4	e5
9.	e1	f2	f3	f4	e5
10.	e1	f2	f3	e4	e5
11.	e1	f2	e3	d4	e5
12.	e1	f2	e3	e4	e5
13.	e1	f2	e3	f4	e5
14.	e1	d2	c3	d4	e5
15.	e1	d2	d3	d4	e5
16.	e1	d2	d3	e4	e5
17.	e1	d2	e3	f4	e5
18.	e1	d2	e3	e4	e5
19.	e1	d2	e3	d4	e5

Solution to Royal Choice

ROYAL CHOICE

How many ways do you think you can move the white king at **e1** to **e5** in only four moves? The simplest is straight ahead: **Ke1 – e2 – e3 – e4 – e5**. More interesting, however, is **Ke1 – d2 – c3 – d4 – e5** or its reverse.

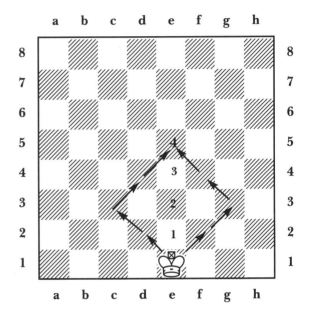

So there are at least three ways. Can you see any more ways to do it? Well, would you believe there are 19 ways…in just four moves!

Try finding some of the ways to get from **e1** to **e4** in just four moves. Find, say, at least seven more ways. Write them down so that you don't repeat ways. When you can't find any more and are ready to give up, turn this page upside down and go through the listing in the box at left to see what paths you've missed.

King and Pawn Vs. King

It's White's move. How does he shepherd his pawn home to **e8** for a queen?

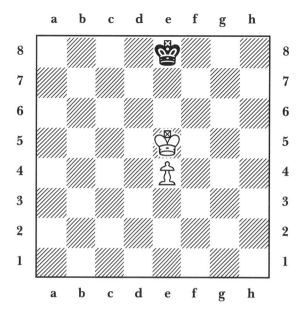

1 Ke5 – e6

White's plan is to control the square on **e8** where his pawn will queen.

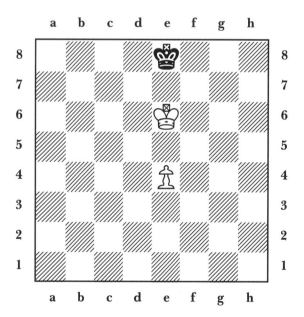

1 ..... Ke8 – d8

The black king has to sidestep to **d8** or **f8**.

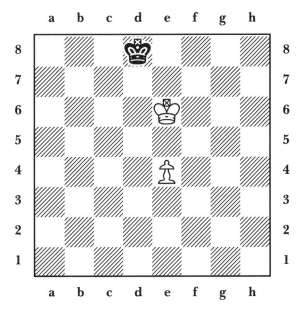

The white king now controls the queening square on **e8**. Will the white pawn now sail through to **e8** and be promoted?

2 Ke6 – f7

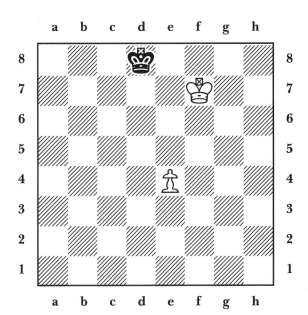

2 ..... Kd8 – d7

The black king tries to stop the white pawn.

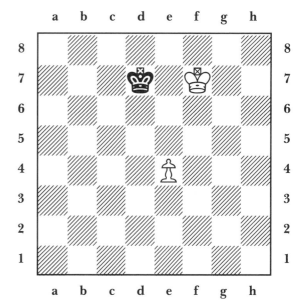

3 e4 – e5

Pawn marches on!

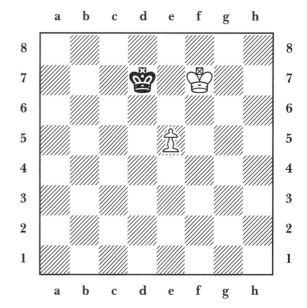

3 ..... Kd7 – c6

The black king is still trying.

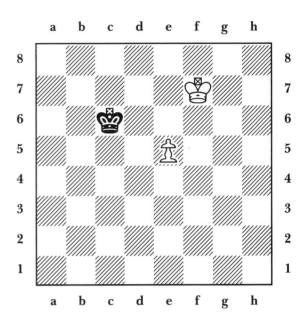

4 e5 – e6

Home run!

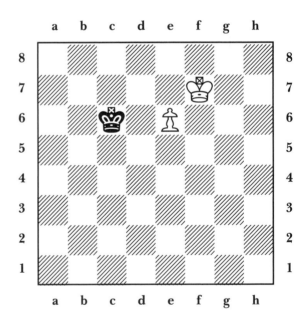

4 ..... Kc6 – d6

Trying to stay close to the white pawn.

5 e6 – e7

Nothing can stop the pawn now.

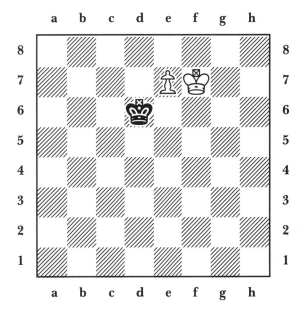

5 ..... Kd6 – d7

But Black is still trying.

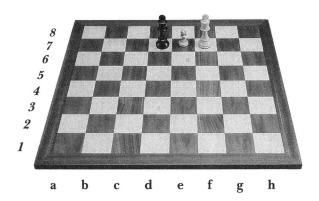

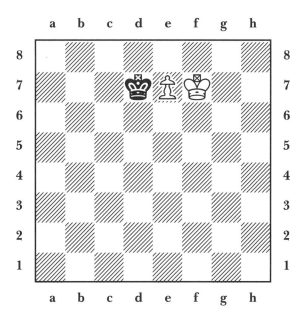

6 e7 – e8(Q)+

The game is won. The black king cannot take the white queen because he would be moving into check from the white king.

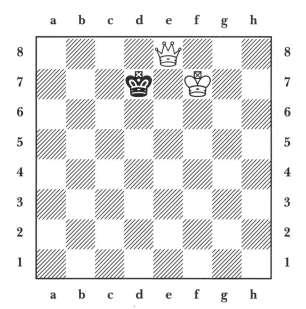

PART FIVE

THE QUEEN

Judith Polgar

Photo by Jami L. Anson, courtesy of U.S. Chess Federation, New Windsor, NY 12553

Presenting
Her Majesty

That here I kiss her as my sovereign Queen.
Shakespeare—*Henry V*

Recap: The queen can move in any straight line—up or down, diagonally, or side to side—as far as she likes. One square, two or more if need be. But no jumping! To take, she lands on a piece. Now, let's see if you can conquer our queen's advanced driving test.

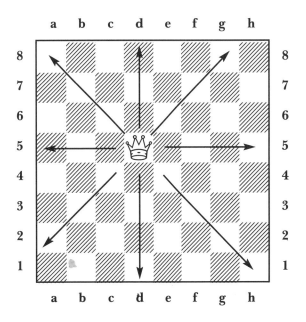

The Queen's Maze

Here is a three-part test. First, the queen has to take eight pieces in eight moves.

Now you are warmed up. For this driving test, the queen has to take ten pieces in ten moves. Try it!

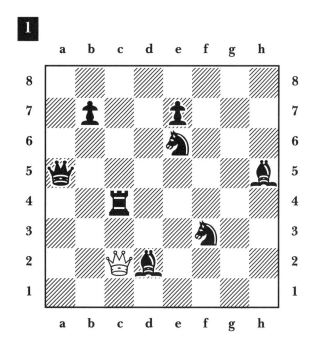

1

2

Try it. You can do it! Then check your solution against the two given below. Did you find a third way?

It probably took you awhile, because, after all, you're not a computer. But did you eventually work it out? Good for you!

Solution **1**: 1.Q×c4 2.Q×e6 3.Q×e7 4.Q×b7 5.Q×f3 6.Q×h5 7.Q×a5 8.Q×d2

Solution **2**: 1.Q×a2 2.Q×a7 3.Q×e7 4.Q×f6 5.Q×g5 6.Q×h4 7.Q×h2 8.Q×b8 9.Q×g8 10.Q×g2

You should have the queen up to speed now. But for this third part, the queen has to take twelve pieces. Let's go!

ONE MORE TIME

Here's an encore: another maze just for good measure…and for the fun of it!

3

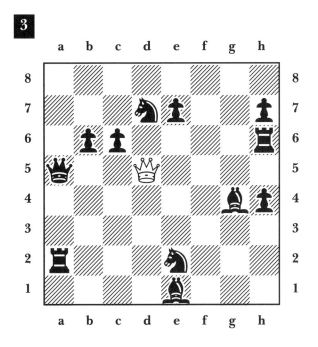

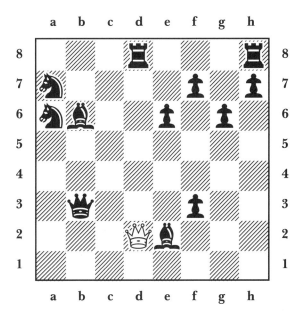

As before, check your solution against the one below. If you have done all three parts correctly, you have passed the test.

Here, again, the white queen takes twelve pieces in twelve moves.

Solution 3: 1. Q × a2 2. Q × e2 3. Q × g4 4. Q × h4 5. Q × h6 6. Q × h7 7. Q × e7 8. Q × e1 9. Q × a5 10. Q × a6 11. Q × c6 12. Q × d7

Solution: 1. Q × d8 2. Q × h8 3. Q × h7 4. Q × g6 5. Q × f7 6. Q × e6 7. Q × b6 8. Q × a7 9. Q × a6 10. Q × e2 11. Q × f3 12. Q × b3

Queen and Pawns Vs. Queen and Pawns

Chess is a game, and there are mini-games to help you learn to play better. In this game, you can practice using a queen to support and advance your pawns. Both queens start on squares of their own color: black queen at **d8** and white queen at **d1**.

Try, with queen and eight pawns each, to be the first to "queen" a pawn.

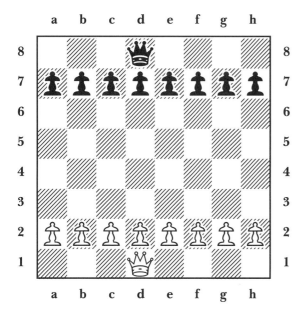

Try these sorts of games as often as you can. Master each piece. Then handling the whole army becomes much easier.

PINNED

When you are working with sharp things like pins, getting stuck can hurt. Getting pinned in chess won't draw blood, but it isn't much fun for you either, so be careful.

Here is an example of a chess pin. Can you see why your white pawn cannot afford to take the black pawn?

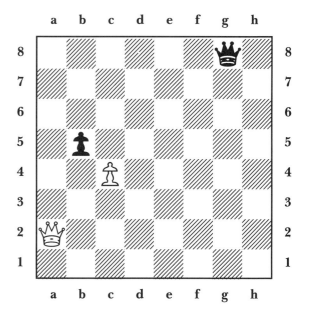

If you take the black pawn, the black queen will take the white one. The white pawn is *pinned* against the white queen.

Or again, here. Why shouldn't your white pawn take the black one?

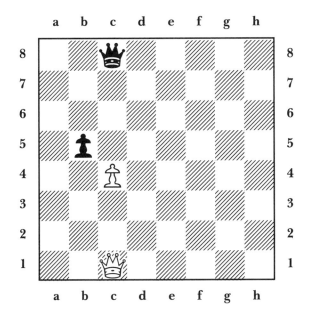

If you could see the results of the take and answered correctly, you have done well. If not, now you know. In both of these examples, the white pawn at **c4** is *pinned*. Moving a pinned piece will very likely lose you a much more valuable piece. Watch for such pins in your games.

Queen of the Café de la Régence

It was summer in the year 1793 and the place was Paris. Citizen Robespierre was striding along to his favorite café, the Café de la Régence. He was chairman of the Revolution, boss of "The Terror," and on his word the young aristocrats, the counts and countesses, went to their death. All the famous men of Paris came to this café, where the chief relaxation was chess. Robespierre, in particular, liked his chess very much.

Just outside Paris a beautiful young girl was crying. Her name was Jacqueline Armand. Her young fiancé, the Duc d'Eltine, had been arrested and quickly sentenced to death. His only crime...being a duke!

Jacqueline was desperate to free her young man. She knew that Robespierre enjoyed chess and played regularly at the café. She also knew that the café was strictly "men only." Cutting off her shoulder-length hair, she dressed as a young man of the Revolution, then went to meet the man who held the lives of many in France in his hands.

Robespierre had just finished a game, but it was his fashion to play all comers. So, as soon as the seat opposite him was free, Jacqueline slipped into it. "And what are the stakes, *mon ami?*" Robespierre asked. He loved to gamble and every game had its price.

"On my part, if I win—a special request. If you win, I will pay the money you say," the stranger responded.

It wasn't too hard for Robespierre to guess

that this game was to be one of life and death, and he was...intrigued. "Accepted," he said, with a smile on his face and more than ever determined to win.

Play proceeded—Robespierre playing White, and Jacqueline Armand playing Black—until, finally, Robespierre pushed his advanced pawn to the far rank, and promoted the piece to a new, second queen:

f7 – f8(Q)

The game had reached this position, with two white queens, and it was Jacqueline's move!

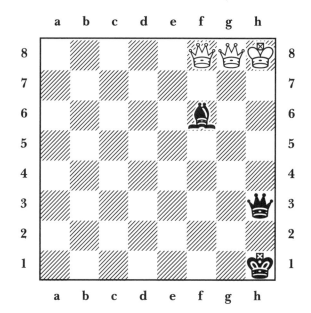

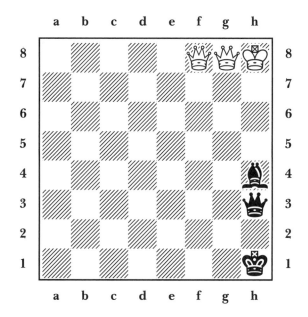

And *there* it was, just waiting for checkmate! (Do you see it?)

Jacqueline played:

..... Bh4 – f6 check

Robespierre was stunned. He was in *double* check: from the bishop and from the queen. In fact, it was double check and checkmate!

Robespierre looked up, now noting the fine, sensitive face of his opponent. "What is your request, young man...or should I say, young *woman*?"

Jacqueline had won, but she had also been found out. Still, her answer came clearly and without a moment of hesitation or concern for her own welfare. "The life of my fiancé, the Duc d'Eltine."

Robespierre gazed across the chess board at the figure sitting straight and unflinching before him. He pondered the request before speaking. "You have been very brave; braver than I should have believed possible here and now, considering...

"Your fiancé," he added finally, "is free."

King and Queen Vs. King

When beggars die there are no comets seen. The heavens themselves blaze forth the death of princes.

Shakespeare—*Julius Caesar*

The ending "king and queen versus king" is very important. It often happens that someone has an extra pawn and promotes it into a queen. It is very embarrassing to be a whole queen up and not know how to win.

Here, the pawn has just reached the other side and become a queen. You have to get checkmate inside fifty of your moves—a special rule. But it should take you much less. If you practice hard, you can even get it down to about ten moves.

We are going to show you, now, such a checkmate, and from one of the hardest positions of king and queen versus a lone king.

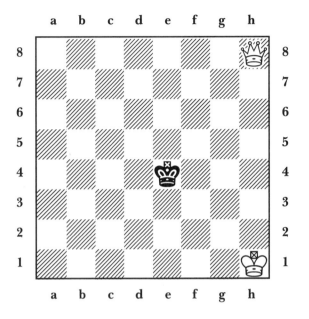

THE FIFTY-MOVE RULE

Even if you have only a king left, you draw if your opponent fails to checkmate you in 50 of his moves. Should, however, something be taken or a pawn be moved, you must go back to 0 and start counting again.

1 Kh1-g2

By itself the queen cannot give checkmate on the open board. The king must help.

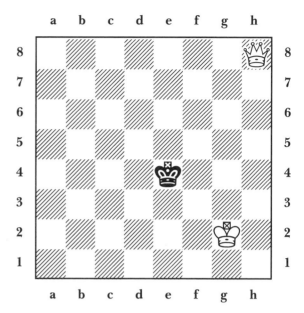

1 ..... Ke4 – d5

The black king wants to stay in the center as long as possible. He has so many moves in the center, it would be impossible to checkmate him there! He can be checkmated only on the edge of the board.

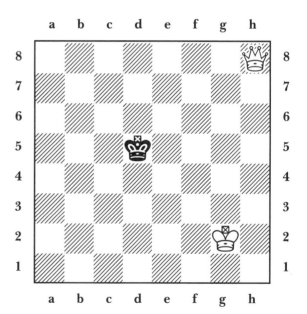

2 Kg2 – f3

The white king is needed, so it continues to head straight for the action! Steinitz said the "king is a fighting piece." The checkmate comes remarkably quickly if the king is properly used.

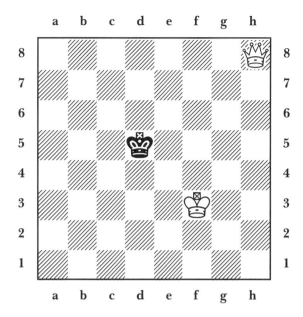

2 ..... Kd5 – c4

The black king tries to stay in the center, where he cannot be mated.

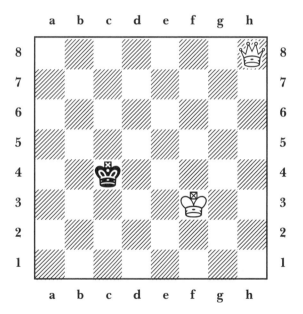

3 Kf3 – e4

The white king continues his march against the black king.

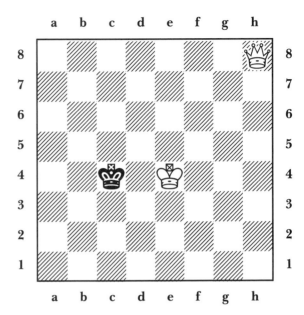

3 ..... Kc4 – c5

Gradually the black king is pushed back to the edge of the board.

4 Qh8 – b2

The white king can't advance, so in comes the
queen to cut off more of the black king's space.

Remember, the king can't move onto squares
covered by enemy pieces, or even by the enemy
king. This would be moving into check.

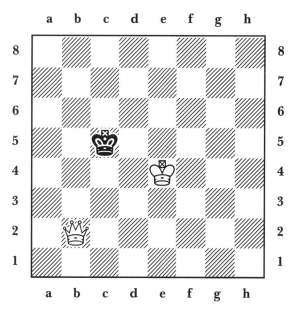

4 ..... Kc5 – c4

Now the two kings are facing each other and
the black king cannot move onto squares beside the white king.

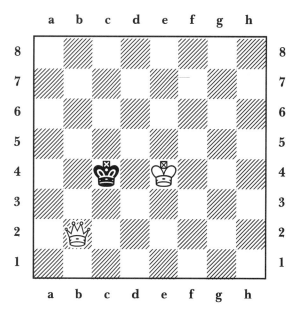

5 Qb2 – c2+

The king is checked. Because of the power of the queen, he cannot stay on the "c" file. He also cannot move toward the black king.

So back he goes!

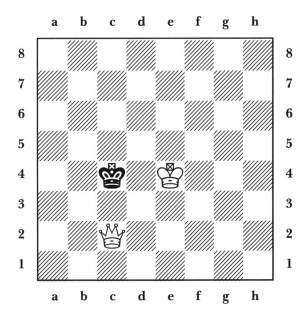

5 ..... Kc4 – b4

With this move, the black king has only the "b" file and the "a" file open to him.

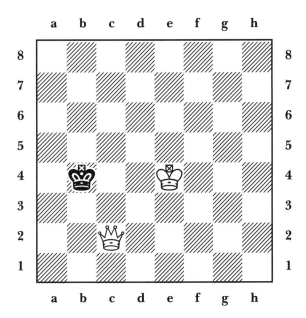

6 Ke4 – d5

The king moves forward again.

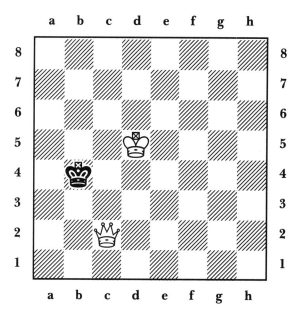

6 ..... Kb4 – b5

And now the black king's path to the "c" file is totally blocked by the white king's command of the squares **c4**, **c5**, and **c6**.

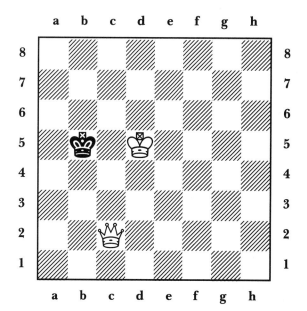

7 Qc2 – b3+

The queen gives check. The king is pushed
back onto the "a" file.

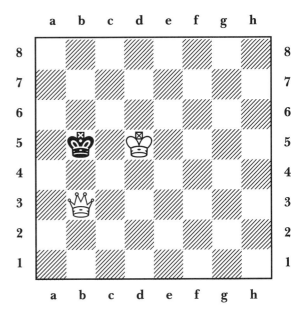

7 ..... Kb5 – a6

The king is driven to the edge of the board,
where nearly half his moves disappear and
checkmate can be given.

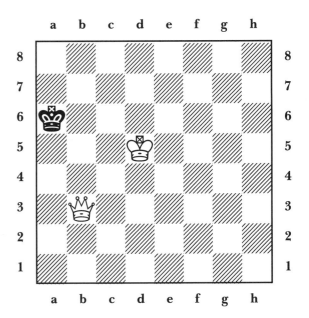

8 Kd5 – c6

The white king muscles in, the move blocking
the approaches to the "b" file. The queen cuts
off the "b" file as well.

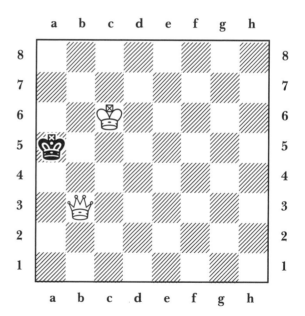

8 ..... Ka6 – a5

There is no way out now!

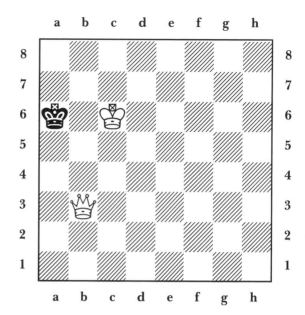

9 Qb3 – b5 checkmate

Now every square to which the king can move is covered by the white queen or king. The black king can't take the queen. It's protected by the white king. It's checkmate. White has won.

The move **Qb3 – a3** would also have been checkmate. And, on his previous move, if the black king had gone to **a7,** then the white queen would simply have mated on **b7**! The king could not escape.

CHECKMATE!

Always remember that the goal of chess is CHECKMATE! Checkmate ends the game. The winner is the player who checkmates the other player's king.

Here is another example of checkmate:

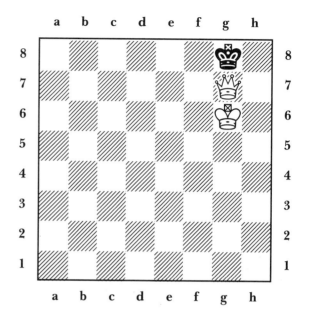

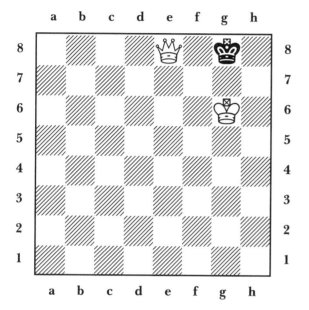

The black king cannot move to **f8** or **h8** because of the white queen. He cannot go to **f7**, **h7,** or to **g7** and take the queen because those squares are covered by the white king. This is not allowed. So this, too, is checkmate.

Let's look at this example:

❖ The white queen attacks the king.
❖ The king cannot step sideways to **f8** or **h8** as the queen also attacks those squares.
❖ The king cannot step forward onto a square covered by the other king. It's not allowed.

The king has no way out—it's checkmate! White has won.

When He Was Eight, Paul Morphy

I never knew so young a body with so old a head.
Shakespeare—*The Merchant of Venice*

As evening fell in long ago New Orleans and the warm daytime temperatures dropped, the logs in the fireplace of Judge Alonzo Morphy's house glowed. Alonzo was playing his brother Ernest at their weekly game of chess. Watching the game closely was Alonzo's eight-year-old son Paul. The two men ignored him. The boy knew the names of the pieces but that was all, they thought.

The game was over and Paul's Uncle Ernest had left, on his way home, when Paul suddenly spoke up, "You made a bad mistake in that game, Father. You could have won."

Alonzo Morphy, packing away and tidying the night's debris, was only half listening. The boy repeated, "Father, you could have won!" Alonzo frowned. He couldn't remember such a position and was sure his son couldn't either.

Quickly, the boy emptied the box of pieces his father had just packed away, and set up again the position where his father had made his fatal mistake.

Alonzo took in the position again, this time baffled by the child's grasp of the game. "You had better go to bed, Paul," was all he said.

His wife was still awake when he went to bed. "Did you know" he asked, "that we have a new chess player in the family?"

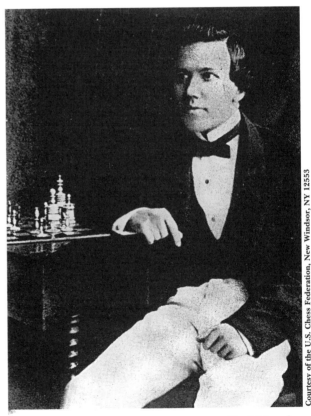

Paul Morphy

Courtesy of the U.S. Chess Federation, New Windsor, NY 12553

Morphy at Twenty-One

In Paris in 1858, at the age of just twenty-one, Paul Morphy defeated German mathematics professor Adolf Anderssen, considered the strongest chess player in the world, by seven games to two. Although Morphy was clearly the world champion, the title was unofficial.

With Morphy we come across a life and a career uncannily similar to Bobby Fischer's a century or more later. There are striking parallels. At about the age of twelve both men, in Fischer's words, "got good" at chess. Morphy in New Orleans, a city with a serious passion for chess then, beat the visiting Hungarian grandmaster, Johann Lowenthal, two games to zero in a match of three. At the same age, Fischer was beating all comers at the Manhattan Chess Club in New York City.

When Morphy left America to take on the world's best chess players, the results were as dazzling as those of Fischer. In London, at the age of twenty, Morphy beat all comers in individual games, consultation games against two or more players, and even "handicapped" games, in which he took off his queen's rook. The games from this period remain as fresh and bright as they were over a hundred years ago. One American player compared playing against Morphy to a sensation as strange as an "electric shock, or first love."

The New York Match

We illustrate Morphy's play with a match game against John Schulten in New York City in 1857. Morphy attacks, with every move counting.

	WHITE Schulten	BLACK Morphy
1	e2 – e4	e7 – e5
2	f2 – f4	d7 – d5
3	e4 × d5	e5 – e4
4	Nb1 – c3	Ng8 – f6
5	d2 – d3	Bf8 – b4

This last move above by Morphy pins White's knight, which cannot move because the white king would be left in check. Now, of course, this pinned knight cannot help out in the center.

6 Bc1 – d2, unpinning

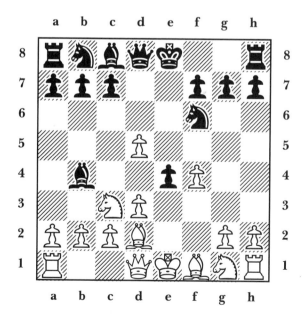

6 ..... e4 – e3

A Morphy move! He wants to open the "e" file and attack down it.

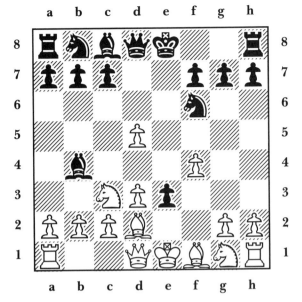

7 Bd2 × e3

Of course! But notice that the knight is now pinned again.

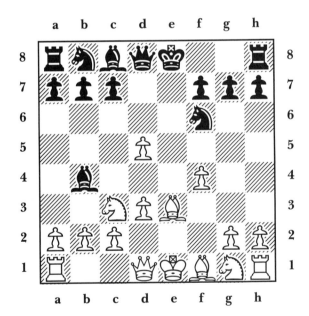

7 ..... O – O

Black castles, and is now ready to put his rook on the same file as the white king. He already has more pieces out than White does.

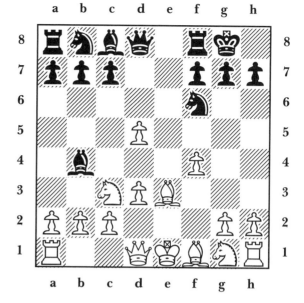

8 Be3 – d2

The white bishop unpins the knight again.

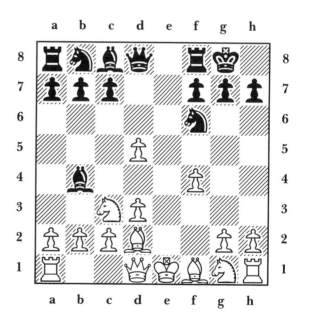

8 ..... Bb4 × c3

This knight is taken off so it cannot block the wide-open "e" file at **e4** or **e2**.

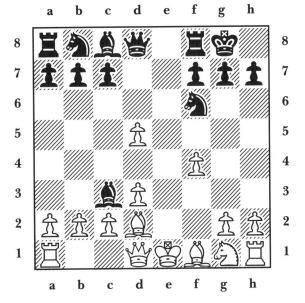

9 b2 × c3

The pawn recaptures.

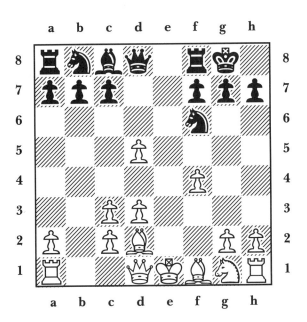

9 ..... Rf8 – e8+

Morphy's rook takes control of the wide-open "e" file.

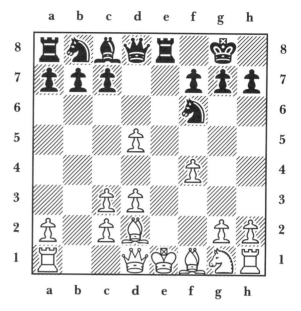

10 Bf1 – e2

The bishop shields the king.

10 ..... Bc8 – g4

Morphy's bishop races out confident that it cannot be taken. Why not? White's bishop is pinned against the king by Black's rook. John Schulten knows that he is facing a Morphy attack.

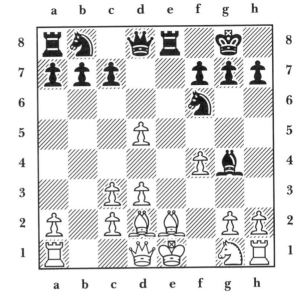

11 c3 – c4

White tries to keep his extra pawns, but it is a bad idea. Far better is to bring his sleeping pieces off the back rank into the action.

11 ..... c7 – c6

Morphy now wants the "d" file open and his other knight in play.

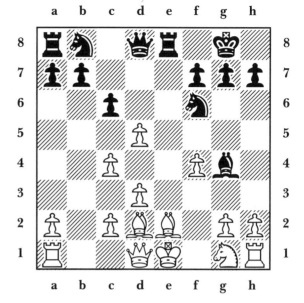

12 d5 × c6

White stays two pawns ahead. But now Black's other knight appears in the attack for the first time. Cavalry reinforcements!

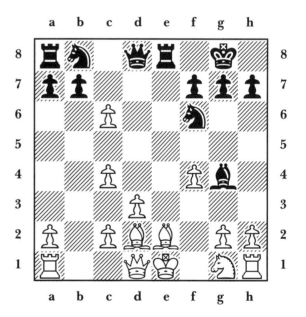

12 ..... Nb8 × c6

Now the threat is **Nc6 – d4**, making the attack on the king even stronger. It is now difficult for White to find any good defense.

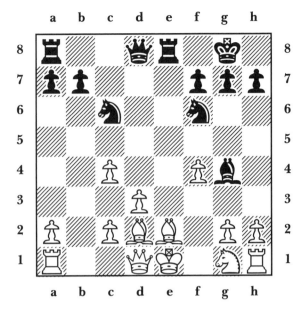

13 Ke1 – f1

The king gets off the dangerous "e" file...but it is too late.

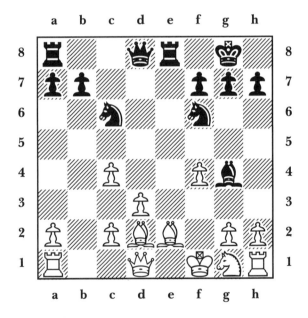

13 ..... Re8 × e2

A typical Morphy move. The pinned bishop had a defender—the knight. Morphy now moves swiftly to bring in another attacker. This newly pinned piece, the knight, has no defenders. Over and over again, this exploiting of the pin is a theme of Morphy's play. Can you guess which piece now joins the attack?

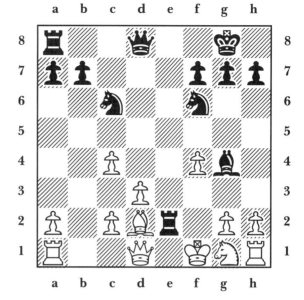

14 Ng1 × e2

Of course! White cannot use his queen to recapture. It is too valuable. Black's bishop would simply take it.

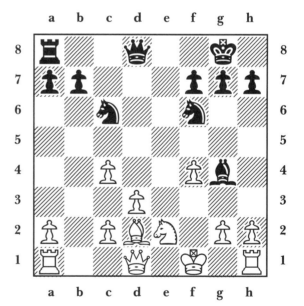

14 ..... Nc6 – d4

You guessed it! Morphy brings another piece to attack the pinned white knight, which is now helpless. If the knight did move, then Morphy would take the white queen.

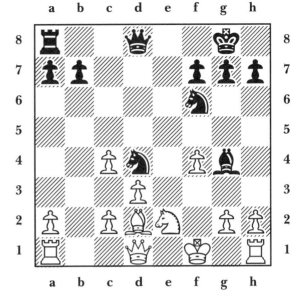

15 Qd1 – b1

The queen moves out of the way. She cannot save the white knight, so she tries to save herself!

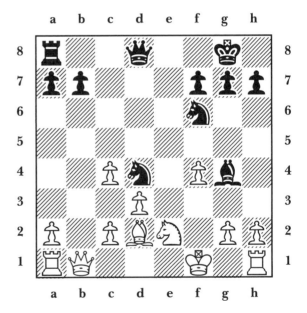

15 ..... Bg4 × e2+

The black bishop snaps up the unprotected knight and gives check.

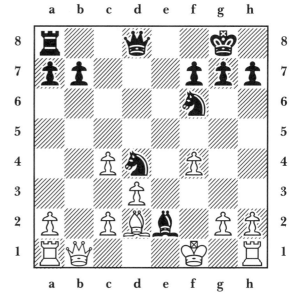

16 Kf1 – f2

The white king's life is now short. All his moves lead to checkmate.

16 ..... Nf6 – g4+

Another black piece joins Morphy's attack, giving check.

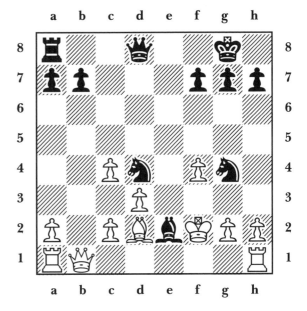

17 Kf2 – g1

The white king hides in the corner. The white king and queen block their own rooks!

17 ..... Nd4 – f3+

The knight sacrifices itself to make way for the deadly black queen. White *must* capture this self-sacrificing knight. It's White's only move to get out of check!

18 g2 × f3

White captures the knight—and now beware!

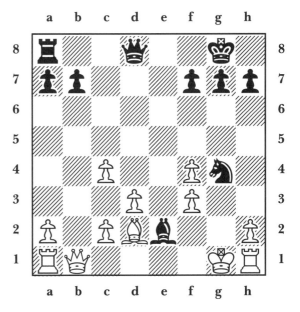

18 ..... Qd8 – d4+

In comes the deadly black queen to a position that Morphy brilliantly fashioned for her.

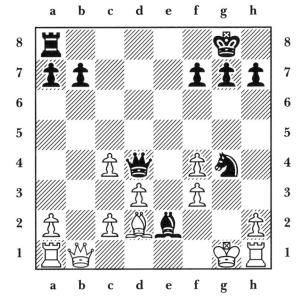

19 Kg1 – g2

Forced!

19 ..... Qd4 – f2+

The black queen strikes into the heart of the
White defense and gives check.

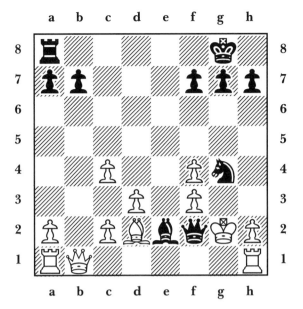

20 Kg2 – h3

The king escapes—but not for long!

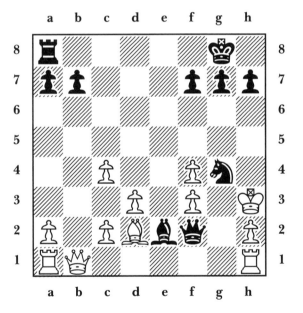

20 ..... Qf2 × f3+

Another damaging check! There's no shelter.
The king is being forced up the board.

21 Kh3 – h4

The white king runs, but he cannot hide!

21 ..... Ng4 – h6

The knight moves from **g4** to allow the queen to come and give checkmate.

22 Qb1 – g1

The white queen makes its second move of the game, coming to stop the checkmate at **g4**.

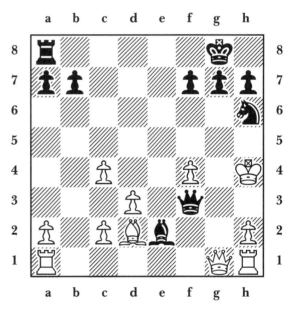

22 ..... Nh6 – f5+

The knight gives the next-to-last check.

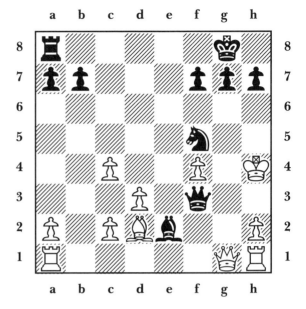

23 Kh4 – g5

His majesty's last move.

23 ..... Qf3 – h5 checkmate

Morphy has played the attack with every move counting!

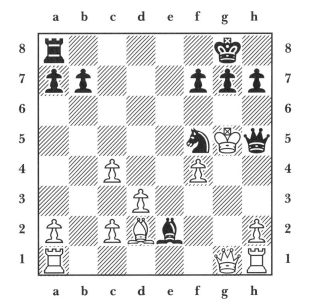

Photo by George C. Koranyi, courtesy of the U.S. Chess Federation, New Windsor, NY 12553

When He Was Eighteen, Bobby Fischer

In 1961, the American Chess Federation with the help of a member of the Rothschild family, Mrs. Jacqueline Piatigorsky, put up a purse of some eight thousand dollars for a match between two noted New York players: Sammy Reshevsky, who had been for some time one of the greatest match players in the world, and the eighteen-year-old sensation Robert J. (Bobby) Fischer. The match ended when, at five and a half points each, Fischer walked out—the first of many such incidents in his strange career.

The walkout was a shame, because the games were so marvelous. Reshevsky's victories in the first and seventh games fulfilled the magnificent promise he first showed at the tender age of seven. Fischer's smashing of Reshevsky's Sicilian Defense in the second game demonstrated his beautiful attacking style and his mastery with King's Pawn openings.

Bobby Fischer

Courtesy www.chesscafe.com

Fischer then gave an interview, with Ralph Ginsberg of *Harper's Magazine*, in which he claimed to be the best player who ever lived. It was a boast, but one he continued to match with his deeds. At Bled in, what was then Yugoslavia, Fischer came through a tournament with Russian giants Mikhail Tal and Tigran Petrosian undefeated. Fischer beat them both. He demolished their colleague Efim Geller in about twenty moves. Fischer then went to Stockholm, Sweden, and again took on the world's best. This time he finished nearly three points ahead of everyone. One month before his nineteenth birthday, he stood at the summit of world chess.

If you look at our ratings chart (pages 112–113), you will see how quickly Fischer improved. Maybe you can do it, too. Who knows?

Photo by George C. Koranyi, courtesy of the U.S. Chess Federation, New Windsor, NY

♟ ♟ **DID YOU KNOW?** ♟ ♟

Ten-year-old Sammy Reshevsky, playing in a strong New York City tournament in 1922, beat David Janowski, a former world championship contender. In 1845, when future American champion Paul Morphy was only eight, he was already touring chess clubs to play simultaneous games on many boards.

Give Yourself a Rating

Comparisons are odorous.

Shakespeare—*Much Ado About Nothing*

Nowadays, nearly all sports—including tennis, golf, football, baseball, and cricket—rate their players. The game of chess was the first to have a rating system for its players. The highest-graded player in the history of chess is Gary Kasparov, who has recently surpassed Bobby Fischer's 2800.

How about your rating? Even though you may be only a beginner, by passing all the tests given in this book, and gaining the certificate we've provided, you can give yourself an international rating of 1000.

Then, this is the system for rating your play:

❖ If you win, take your opponent's grade and add 400.
❖ If you lose, take your opponent's grade and subtract 400.
❖ If you draw, take your opponent's grade.
❖ The average of all the results, including your original 1000 rating, is your grade.

Note: If, however, you lose to somebody who is graded much higher than you, you are not allowed to gain points by losing! For example, if you were to play Bobby Fischer, you are not allowed to take his grade of 2800, subtract 400, and therefore have a grade of 2400.

Similarly, if you beat somebody with a much lower rating than yourself, you are not allowed to lose points by such a win. For example, if you beat a friend who is graded 400, by adding 400 you will have a grade of only 800—so you would be losing 200 grade points. You are not allowed to lose points by winning!

For example:

You win against a player rated 1000 (he has passed all the tests in this book).

1000 + 400 = 1400

Your new rating is 1400.

You then draw a player rated 1200.

1200 + 1400 = 2600

Divide 2600 by 2 = 1300

Your new rating is 1300.

Soon, you and your friends will find yourselves with an international rating! Then you can look at the age progress ratings chart provided on the following pages and see how you compare with Kasparov, Fischer, Morphy, and other top chess players.

Age/Rating Progress: A Chart

Rating	1700	1800	1900	2000	2100	2200	2300
Ages							

World Champions

Name		1700	1800	1900	2000	2100	2200	2300
Morphy	(1858)							
Steinitz	(1866–94)							
Lasker	(1894–1921)							
Capablanca	(1921–27)				12	13	13	17
Alekhine	(1927–35, '37–45)				14	14	14	14
Euwe	(1935–37)				14		16	18
Botvinnik	(1948–57, '58–60, '61–63)			13	13	13	13	
Smyslov	(1957–58)							
Tal	(1960–61)						15	
Petrosian	(1963–69)							
Spassky	(1969–72)	10	12	11	11	12	13	14
Fischer	(1972–75)							12
Karpov	(1975–85, '93–)	8	8	9	10	11	12	13
Kasparov	(1985–)				10	11	12	13

Contemporary Grandmasters

Name		1700	1800	1900	2000	2100	2200	2300
Viswanathan Anand	(India, Dec. 11, 1969)							
Gata Kamsky	(U.S.A., June 2, 1974)							13
Nigel Short	(England, June 1, 1965)	9	9	10	10	11	12	14
Judith Polgar	(Hungary, July 23, 1976)							10

Top Juniors

Name		1700	1800	1900	2000	2100	2200	2300
Sergei Movsesian	(Armenia, July 18, 1977)							14
Thien Hai Dao	(Vietnam, May 10, 1978)					13		
Ruslan Ponomariov	(Ukraine, Oct. 11, 1983)							12
Etienne Bacrot	(France, Jan. 22, 1983)						10	11
Luke McShane	(England, Jan. 7, 1984)					9	11	12

Information provided in parentheses: World Champions' years of reign (Karpov and Kasparov, both of Russia, have each been recognized world champion by separate organizations since 1993); Contemporary Grandmasters' and Top Juniors' native country and birth date.
Information collected by Bob Wade. Chart compiled by Allan Lewis.

2400	2450	2500	2550	2600	2650	2700	2750	Rating (7/1/98)
						21		–
	24	26	29	32				–
			20	21		30	46	–
17		18		20		24	32	–
15		19		25		35	39	–
19	20	22	24	27	34			–
14	14	15	19	20	22	27	30	–
	15		19		24	31		–
16	17	18	19	21		22		–
15		18	21	26	31			–
15		16		18		28		–
13		14	15	16	18	20	27	–
15		17		20		23	25	2725
15		17	20	21		22		2815
		17	18	20	21	23	27	2795
		15			16	20		2720
15		17	20	21	23			2670
			12	16	19			2665
16	16		17	17				2640
			14					2580
			13					2585
12	13	13						2555
	13							2470

A World Chess (FIDE) Master is rated at 2300. An International Master is rated at 2400, and a Grandmaster at 2500.

It would not be right to complete this table without a mention of Sammy Reshevsky, the most famous of all chess prodigies. At the age of seven, he was already rated at 2000. Sammy came to New York from Poland in 1920 when he was nine. He could already play chess blindfolded. He was soon befriended by the great Hollywood star Charlie Chaplin. At the age of ten, he beat David Janowski, who had once played a world title match against Emanuel Lasker. Sammy's parents then made him give up chess and concentrate on his education. When Reshevsky came back to play in his twenties, he was acknowledged as one of the best match players in the world. Some felt he was even the *very* best.

It would also be wrong not to point out the phenomenal progress of Judith Polgar, born July 23, 1976. At the age of ten, she was already rated 2300, making Judith and young Sammy Reshevsky the strongest ten-year-old players ever. At fifteen, Judith became the youngest grandmaster, younger even than world champions Fischer or Kasparov were when winning the title.

Net That King!

Progressive chess is a game that also teaches you how to build mating nets around opponents' kings.

In this game, the number of moves is progressive. White starts with one move, but then Black has two moves in a row. Then White has three moves, Black four…and so on.

There are two more *special* rules:

1. You are allowed to give check *only* on the *last* of your series of moves.
2. You must get *out of check* on the *first* of your moves.

What do you think? Does it sound like fun… or what! Maybe it just depends on who, exactly, you are playing!

BOB WADE, O.B.E.*, PLAYS PROGRESSIVE CHESS

Bob Wade, one of the authors of this book, is one of the world's greatest chess scholars.

Bob has traveled to nearly every corner of the world in the cause of spreading the game of chess. He is now eager to go to Namibia, in Africa—one of the few countries he has not yet visited.

Here, Bob Wade gives a game played under progressive chess rules against a mystery player on a train journey in Canada. In the game that follows, Bob duels unsuccessfully against a mystery opponent on a train. Who was it? The great Fischer himself? Someone—some*thing*—more…sinister? Perhaps even the Devil himself? Judge for yourself!

*The letters "O.B.E." after his name designate a very special honor Bob Wade was given by the Queen of England—named "Officer of the Order of the British Empire."

Lost on a Train

Bob has the white pieces and plays first, a single move. His play is:

1 e2–e4 (1 move)

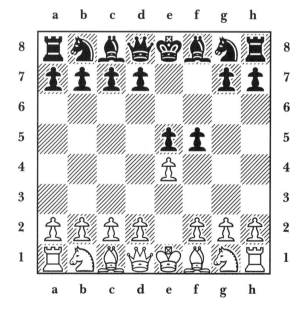

The excitement mounts. According to the rules, the mystery player, playing Black, now has two moves. Black plays:

1 ..... e7–e5 and **..... f7–f5** (2 moves)

Progressive chess is a cause for nail biting. By the rules of the game, Bob has now three moves, and he is ready. Bob plays:

2 d2–d4, f2–f4 and **Bf1–c4** (3 moves)

The mystery player, playing Black, studies his opponent, an International Master, then the board. He has four moves.

A moment later, a slow smile. He knows his strength. He will get his queen to **g2**. Just two moves will be needed. Black plays:

2 ..... Qd8–g5, ... Qg5–g2 ... (2 moves)

Look. The black queen now covers all the white king's four escape squares! But another piece is required to deliver the checkmate. Can you see which one of his pieces the mystery player will choose?

Remember, the check/checkmate has to be delivered *on the last move*. The mystery player has two moves left of his four in this progressive game.

He makes his selection, and with devilish force he moves…the black bishop. It can deliver check and checkmate.

… **….. Bf8–e7** and then **….. Be7–h4**
(for a total of 4 moves)

The king has no escape squares because of the queen at **g2**. The checking bishop cannot be blocked. It is checkmate! Was Bob playing the Devil?

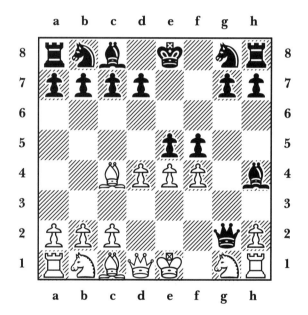

PART SEVEN

THE END...AND THE BEGINNING

In reading through this book and doing the tests and mazes we've provided, you have learned a lot about chess players—from the famous chess-playing codebreakers of wartime England to the top masters of today—and the old but still exciting game of chess.

There is more to learn, including tried-and-true tactics and new strategies of the game. But what you have already learned here is a good start, and we feel that you deserve something tangible to attest to your accomplishments so far. That is why we give you, here, a certificate that you can have filled out and signed by a parent, chess teacher, or other authority, and put up in your room—among the other chess trophies and awards that you are sure to win if you keep learning and playing chess.

Following the certificate, we have included a summary of the rules of chess, made available to us by the U.S. Chess Federation. If you continue to play chess, you will hear a lot about this organization, and the chess tournaments that it sponsors. We would not be surprised to hear that you, and our other readers, are taking part in them and making a good showing. In fact, we expect you to. But, first, we expect you to enjoy playing chess.

Photos by Jim Woodward, Sebastian Studios, courtesy USCF, New Windsor, NY 12553

CERTIFICATE OF ACHIEVEMENT

This is to certify that _____

having read the book *Winning Chess Piece by Piece*, and

completed and passed its mazes and challenges, including:

- ☐ Rook's Maze
- ☐ Rook's Mill Test 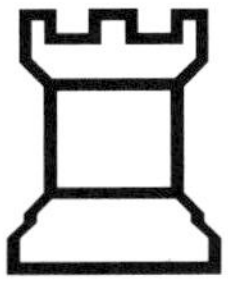
- ☐ Knight's Maze
- ☐ Bishop's Maze 
- ☐ Queen's Maze
- ☐ Penrose Knight-Fork Memory Test

has earned this honorable

Certificate of Achievement, signed and hereby

presented by the authors:

Ted Nottingham,
Bob Wade
and Al Lawrence

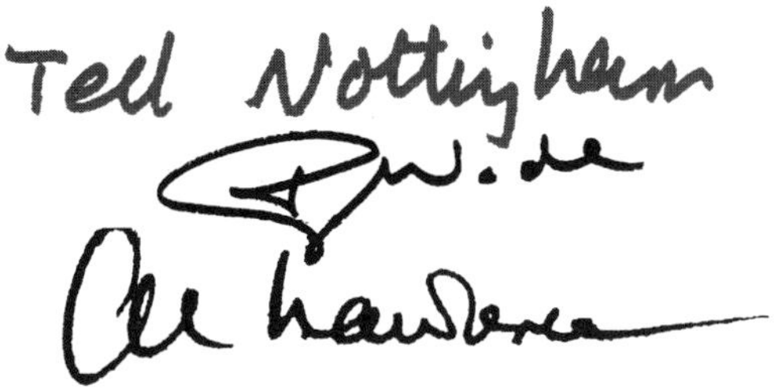

Ted Nottingham
Bob Wade
Al Lawrence

Attested to and signed by:

_____   _____
Name   Date

USCF's *Let's Play Chess**:
A Review

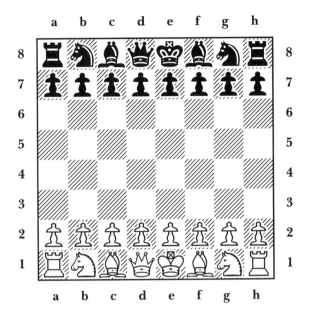

Chess is a game for two players: White using white pieces and Black using black pieces. At the start of the game, the pieces are set up as shown at right.

Here are hints to help you remember the proper board setup:

❖ The opposing kings and queens go directly opposite each other.

❖ The square in the lower right-hand corner is a light one ("light on right").

❖ The white queen goes on a light square, the black queen goes on a dark square ("queen on color").

THE PIECES—HOW THEY MOVE

White always moves first, and then the players take turns moving. Only one piece may be moved at each turn (except for "castling"— a special move explained later). The knight is the only piece that can jump over other pieces. All other pieces move only along unblocked lines. You may not move a piece to a square already occupied by one of your own pieces. But you can capture, or take, an "enemy" piece that stands on a square where one of your pieces can move. Simply remove the enemy piece from the board and put your own piece in its place.

The King is the most important piece in chess play. When he is trapped, his whole army loses. The king can move one square in any direction—for example, to any of the dotted squares

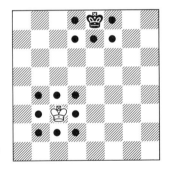

in this diagram. (Castling is an exception.) The king may never move into check—that is, onto a square that is being attacked by an opponent's piece.

*This quick-reference *Let's Play Chess* has been provided courtesy of the U.S. Chess Federation, New Windsor, N.Y. 12553. It has been adapted and is printed here with the Federation's permission.

The Queen is the most powerful piece. She can move any number of squares in any direction—horizontal, vertical, or diagonal—as long as her path is not blocked. In the position at right, she can reach any of the dotted squares in the diagram.

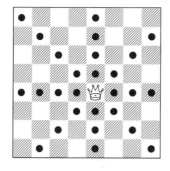

The Rook is the next-most-powerful piece. It can move any number of squares, either vertically or horizontally, as long as its path is not blocked.

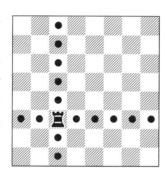

The Bishop can move any number of squares diagonally if its path is not blocked. Note that this bishop starts on a light square and can reach only other light squares. At the start of the game, you have one "dark-square" bishop and one "light-square" bishop.

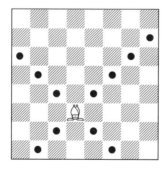

The Knight's move is special. It hops directly from its old square to its new one. The knight can jump over other pieces between its old and its new squares. Think of the knight's move as an "L." It moves two squares horizontally or vertically and then makes a right-angle turn for one more square. The knight always lands on a square opposite in color from its old square.

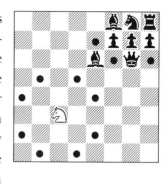

The Pawn's move is straight ahead (never backwards) but it captures diagonally. It moves one square at a time, except on its first move, when it has the option of moving forward one or two squares. Here, the squares with dots indicate possible destinations for the pawns. The white pawn is on its original square, so it may move ahead either one or two squares. The black pawn has already moved, so it may move ahead only one square at a time. The squares on which these pawns may capture are indicated by an X. If a pawn advances to the opposite end of the board, it is immediately "promoted" to another piece, usually a queen. It may not remain a pawn or become a king. Therefore, it is possible for each player to have more than one queen, or more than two rooks, bishops, or knights on the board at the same time.

SPECIAL MOVES

Castling may be done by each player only once during a game and only when certain conditions are met. It is a special move that lets a player move two pieces at once: the king and one rook. In castling, the player moves his king two squares to its left or right, toward one of its rooks. At the same time, the rook involved goes to the square beside the king and toward the center of the board. In order to castle, neither the king nor the rook involved may have moved before. Also, the king may not castle out of check, into check, or through check. Further, there may not be pieces of either color between the king and the rook involved in castling. Castling is often a very important move because it allows you to place your king in a safe location and also allows the rook to become more active. When the move is legal, each player has the choice of castling kingside or queenside or not at all—no matter what the other player chooses to do.

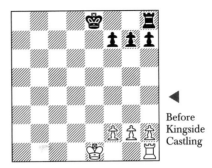

Before
Kingside
Castling

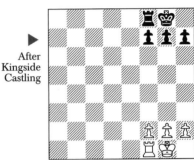

After
Kingside
Castling

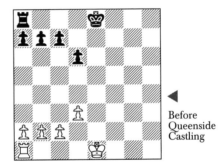

Before
Queenside
Castling

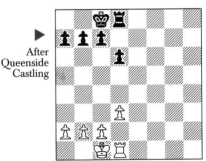

After
Queenside
Castling

En passant is French for "in passing." This phrase is used for a special pawn capture. It occurs when one player moves a pawn two squares forward to try to avoid capture by the opponent's pawn.

The capture is made exactly as if the player had moved the pawn only one square forward. In the diagram above, the black pawn moves up two squares to the square with the dot. On its turn, the white pawn may capture the black one on the square marked with the X. If the white player does not exercise this option immediately—before playing some other move—the black pawn is safe from "en passant" capture for the rest of the game. But new opportunities may arise for each pawn in similar circumstances.

ABOUT CHECK AND CHECKMATE

The main goal of chess is to checkmate your opponent's king. The king is not actually captured and removed from the board like other pieces. But if the king is attacked ("checked") and threatened with capture, it must get out of check immediately. If there is no way to get out of check, the position is a "checkmate," and the side that is checkmated loses. You may not move into check: For example, moving into a direct line with your opponent's rook, if there are no other pieces between the rook and your king, is not a legal move. Otherwise, the rook could "capture" the king, which is not allowed. If you are in check, there are three ways of getting out:

❖ Capture the attacking piece.
❖ Place one of your own pieces between the attacker and your king (unless the attacker is a knight).
❖ Move the king away from the attack.

If a checked player can do none of these, he is checkmated and loses the game. If a king is not in check, but that player can make no legal move, the position is called a *stalemate* and the game is scored as a *draw*, or tie.

Our Handsome Commander

For there never was a tale of more woe.
Shakespeare—*Romeo and Juliet*

The first leaves are falling in the autumn of 1942. President Franklin D. Roosevelt is being pushed in his wheelchair in the rose garden of Hyde Park, his home on the Hudson River north of New York City. He has just viewed some disturbing photographs. Across the Atlantic, Prime Minister Winston Churchill has seen them, too. Solemnly, these two powerful world leaders issue a joint statement, with the Russians, warning the Nazis about their war crimes against Jews and others.

In Warsaw, Poland, a young girl writes in her diary about Mordechai Anielewicz "our handsome commander whom we all love." But she knows that soon, in the ghetto, he and many others—possibly she too—will soon die. Mordechai, although he has only two revolvers, is pledged to fight. He is training his young men to fire the guns.

It is sad history now. Mordechai and many young people were among those to die fighting in the ghetto. With their pitiful arsenal, they managed to defy an S.S. brigade for thirty-three days—leaving the world an imperishable symbol of defiance. They were overwhelmed, at the end, only when their buildings were set ablaze, burning the Polish fighters out. During their resistance, sometime before he died, Mordechai wrote, "In all our dugouts there is not enough air to light a single candle." It was a shocking waste of life and young talent.

But, in the midst of all the suffering, Jerzy Prezpiorka, a chess grandmaster also trapped in the ghetto, has an idea. To lift morale, he suggests a display of his skills. He will play all comers. Mordechai agrees, and a chess set is improvised out of glue and bits of wood. In the ghetto, usually nobody could think of anything but food and danger but, on that day, many come to watch. If only for a brief moment, they are lifted out of their misery. Mordechai, the young girl's "handsome commander," speaks to the people gathered. He takes a moment to remind them that not all Germans are Nazis. That it was a German, Siegbert Tarrasch, who once said, "Chess, like love, like music, has the power to make men happy."

THE BOOK IS ENDED

The book is ended and so is the game.
But I have gained a pleasing fame.
I found my thinking much improved
Because I learnt a certain move.
My queen was cornered.
My king was checked.
I was trapped and began to fret.
But I used my skill and planned a scheme,
Turning Rose's face quite green.
I beat Mary, lost to Sally —
And found a pleasant friend in Harry!

Phyllis Woodall

INDEX

Whether you play chess for fun or chess for blood... Whether you're a casual player or a tournament veteran... You're invited to join America's coast-to-coast chess club! We're the U.S. Chess Federation, with over 85,000 members of all ages — from beginners to grandmasters!

U.S. ♔ CHESS
FEDERATION

U.S. Chess Federation membership offers many benefits:

- The right to earn a national rating!
- Big discounts on chess merchandise
- A national magazine packed with information
- An official membership card
- The right to play in local, regional, and national tournaments
- The right to play officially rated chess by mail

☑ Yes! Enroll me as follows:

☐ Adult, $40 (1 year) $75 (2 years)   ☐ Senior (age 65 or older) $30/yr.
☐ Youth (age 19 and under; includes monthly *Chess Life* issue) $17/yr.
☐ Scholastic (age 14 and under; includes bimonthly *School Mates* issue) $12/yr.
☐ **Also, I want my FREE *Play Chess* video (a $19.95 value).**
   I include $4.50 to cover shipping and handling costs.
☐ Send me *Play Chess I Video* (Covers the basics, plus winning strategic tips.) OR
☐ *Play Chess II Video* (Takes beginners who know the moves all the way to their first tournament.)

Check or money order enclosed, in the amount of $_____ or charge it. MasterCard. DISCOVER VISA AMERICAN EXPRESS

Credit card number _____ Expiration date _____

Authorized signature _____
Daytime telephone _____

Name _____
Address _____
City _____ State _____ ZIP _____
Birthdate _____ Sex _____

Call toll free: 800-388-KING (5464) Please mention Dept. 77 when responding.
FAX: 914-561-CHES(2437) or **Mail:** U.S. Chess Federation, Dept. 77
                3054 NYS Route 9W, New Windsor, NY 12553
Visit our website at http://www.uschess.org.

Note: Membership dues are not refundable. Canada: Add $6/yr. for magazine postage & handling. Other foreign: Add $15/yr.